JWK

DESIGNED BY

MARSHALL LEE

A
BALANCE HOUSE
BOOK
PUBLISHED
BY

David R. Godine

BOSTON

JOSEPH WOOD KRUTCH
HERBAL

Published in 1976 by
David R. Godine, Publisher
306 Dartmouth Street
Boston, Massachusetts

Copyright © 1965 by Balance House, New York
ISBN 0-87923-171-8 hardcover
0-87923-165-3 softcover
LCC 65-20676

Printed in the United States of America

For NANCY *and* KENNETH BECHTEL
whose unflagging hospitality made this book possible

The author wishes to acknowledge the aid of the Belvedere Scientific Fund which helped make possible the writing of this book. He is also grateful to the libraries and their staffs at the University of Arizona and at the University of California at Berkeley. The several quotations from *The Book of Beasts,* translated by T. H. White, are used with the kind permission of the publishers, G. P. Putnam's Sons.

For nought so vile upon the earth doth live,
But to the earth some special good doth give.

WILLIAM SHAKESPEARE
Romeo and Juliet, Act II: Scene 3

Contents

The illustrations in this book are taken from the woodcuts in Pierandrea Mattioli's huge folio volume, *Commentaries on the Six Books of Dioscorides,* issued in Prague in 1563 and Venice in 1565. The work was first published in 1544 and appeared in some fifty editions in several languages, but all of those prior to 1563 had very much smaller plates.

It is not known who made all of these monumental drawings and cut them in wood, but most of them are generally attributed to Giorgio Liberale and Wolfgang Meyerpeck. However, on the Orange plate (page 113) the initials WS appear in the lower left corner, indicating that at least one other craftsman was involved. In any case, these are certainly among the finest Herbal illustrations ever printed and are obviously, for the most part, based upon observation rather than being copies of copies, as was so often the practice up to that time.

In the absence of any standardized system of names, the pre-Linnaean Herbalist could not always be sure what plant one of his predecessors (or, for that matter, one of his foreign contemporaries) was talking about—not even when Latin was used. Moreover, he came only gradually to realize that similar species may be numerous, and that the one found growing in England or Germany may be very much, but not quite, the same as one described by an Italian. Sometimes there was a never-resolved dispute concerning even the general type of plant given a certain name by one of the classic authorities.

But despite all these difficulties, the family and genus of the plants represented in the Plates is pretty clear, and these are given, in that order, below each illustration. Where the species is reasonably certain, and of some significance, it is generally named in the text. Each Plate and the commentary facing it is labeled with the plant's common name. In a few cases, the name given is only one of several used at various times and places for the same or similar varieties. Since the origin of popular names is a matter more of poetry than science, some poetic license is claimed in their use.

INTRODUCTION

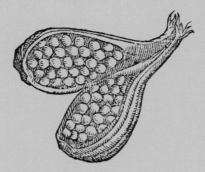

"Many thousands and thousands of perils and dangers beset man. He is not fully sure of his health or his life for one moment . . . but the Creator of Nature who has placed us amid such dangers has mercifully provided us with a remedy—that is, with all kinds of herbs, animals, and other created things to which He has given power and might."

These are the words of an anonymous fifteenth-century German as they were translated by an English contemporary, and set forth in the preface to one of the more important of those treatises on the medicinal plants which are still called Herbals.

Like all of the Herbals in whatever language they happen to be written, this German work takes off from what the author knew of ancient writings in Greek or Latin, and attempts to summarize and combine them with such additions as observation or hearsay could contribute. But as this particular work also clearly illustrates, what they all either imply or state, is a certain metaphysical assumption which our quotation takes for granted: Everything in the universe has a purpose, and that purpose is God's glory, man's welfare or, usually, both. This is equally true of the planets which rain down influences upon us every moment of our lives and of the herbs growing at our feet. Learning leads to wisdom and wisdom consists of the ability to recognize the purpose for which things are intended. Thus botany, for instance, is primarily the art of discovering the special virtue of each plant for the cure of one or another of the ills with which mankind is threatened. Because of these metaphysical assumptions, the few words of the above quotation are sufficient to carry us back across the centuries into a late medieval world, where the very premises of men's thinking seem irreconcilable with our own.

There are two very different ways of looking at any of the many Herbals which lie between that of their chief source, the Greek physician Dioscorides (first century A.D.), and the beginnings of unmistakably modern botany and medicine during the seventeenth and eighteenth centuries. One way—and the most usual—is to see science slowly freeing itself from ignorance, superstition, and false reasoning. Just as alchemy, we say, gave birth to chemistry, so the labors of the Herbalist gave birth to medicine on the one hand and to scientific botany on the other. Regarded thus, they merely document ignorance and folly beginning to yield to knowledge and rationality.

Something from this point of view will presently be said. But there is, as our quotation suggests, another way of considering the significance of the Herbalists. If we dismiss them as merely ignorant and foolish, we get nothing except a sense of superiority and a further confirmation of something we know well enough already—namely, that the blessings conferred by the scientific view are quite recent acquisitions. But if we ask, not how our ancestors could have been so foolish, but rather what is the total meaning of their "quaintness", we may find our imaginations strangely stimulated. Here we enter into a world where the fundamental premises of thoughtful men seem to establish between them and the universe a relationship very different from (and in many ways more reassuring than) either the post-Darwinian or the more recent Existentialist world views.

"WHERE NOTHING GROWS IN VAIN"

The classical writers on botany and other aspects of natural history occasionally adumbrate the main features of this world, but the best of them are much more "scientific" and what we call rational than the medievals are, even though they also are sometimes superstitious and incompletely informed. Theophrastus, a pupil of Aristotle and author of the earliest surviving Greek treatise on plants, often, but not always, comments skeptically on the superstitious beliefs which he records. Pliny, roughly half a millennium later and thus part of the intellectually deteriorating world of Nero's day, is astonishingly uncritical, accepting the wildest unsupported tales as readily as the sober opinions of his more respectable authorities. But superstition affords no more than a hint of the philosophical system which the Herbalists accepted.

This system was a creation of the Middle Ages and, in part, dependent upon the faith of the Christian. It appears quite early and is summarily stated again and again in prefaces or obiter dicta. Though it gradually faded away as its place was taken by the beginnings of our contemporary philosophy of science, it continued to find acceptance in the popular mind long after it had ceased to be considered intellectually respectable. In, for instance, the preface to a 1789 edition of Culpeper's Herbal, then a century and a quarter old, the work is especially recommended because "it resorts for every mode of cure to that infallible source prepared by God and Nature in the vegetable system; whence flows spontaneously the genuine virtues of medicine diffused universally over the face of the earth, where nothing grows in vain".

Or hear what the friar in *Romeo and Juliet* says, speaking for all good renaissance Christians:

> *O! Mickle is the powerful grace that lies*
> *In herbs, plants, stones and their true qualities:*
> *For nought so vile that on the earth doth live*
> *But to the earth some special good doth give.*

"Where nothing grows in vain." Accept that phrase and its implication that the universe is purposeful in every detail as well as in general plan; accept also what few questioned, that man's welfare was the principal end to which this purpose tended, and there was no reason to find anything improbable in what seems to us the most fantastic of the theories derived from it.

THE DOCTRINE OF SIGNATURES

If God created plants to cure men's ills, he would naturally provide clues to guide him in selecting from among them those that tended to relieve the ill from which he was at any moment suffering. Something in their appearance would suggest their intended application and this external clue to an inward virtue came to be known as the herb's "signature". It was, in a way, analogous to the symbols of the Church service in that it too "was an outward and visible sign of an inward and spiritual grace". Reference to some of these signatures survives in both the popular and scientific names of various plants like Hepatica, or Liverwort, which was so called because the shape of the leaves suggested that of the liver, or like Saxifrage, originally given this name because some species which grow among broken rocks plainly indicated that their virtue was to break up gall or kidney stones.

In what survives of classical botany and medicine there is little to suggest that its practitioners took stock in any such notions as are included in the Doctrine of Signatures. But during the Middle Ages the doctrine flourished fantastically. Signatures much more far-fetched than those just cited were readily accepted, and it hung on well into the age of triumphant rationalism. Paracelsus, the early sixteenth-century physician, alchemist and charlatan, carried the doctrine to its furtherest limits as, for instance, in this seventeenth-century English translation of one of his works:

"I have oft times declared how by outward shapes and qualities of things we know their inward virtues which God put in them for the good of man. So in St. John's Wort [the familiar Hypericum of lawn borders and gardens] we may take notice of the forms of the leaves. One. The porosities of the holes in the leaves signify to us that this herb helps both inward or outward holes or cuts in the skin . . . Two. The flowers of St. John's Wort when they are putrified they are like blood which teacheth us that this herb is good for wounds, to close them and fill them up."

By the late seventeenth century, John Ray, who might be called the first English biologist and student of natural history to be almost completely modern in his methods and habits of mind, was rejecting the Doctrine of Signatures out of hand as merely fabulous. But his near contemporary, the herbalist William Coles, was accepting and applying it extensively. Of Hippoglossum, or Horse-tongue, he writes that "the little leaf-like tongue, growing upon the greater, is no light argument that this plant is effectual for sores in the mouth and throat [and] . . . is good for those that have an imperfection in their speech". To Coles, the signature of the walnut is so plain as to be unmistakable. "Walnuts have the perfect signature of the head: the outer husk or green covering represents the Pericranium or outward skin of the skull, whereon the hair groweth, and therefore salts made of those husks or barks are exceedingly good for wounds in the head. The inner woody shell hath the signature of the skull and the little yellow skin or fell that covers the kernel of the hard Meninga and Pia-Mater, which are the thin surfaces which envelop the brain. The kernel hath the very figure of the brain, and therefore it is very preferable for the brain and resists poisons; for if the kernel be bruised and moistened with the quintescence of wine, and laid upon the crown of the head, it comforts the brain and head mightily." Coles was, however, disturbed by the fact that many useful herbs had no obvious signatures and he concluded that while a certain number were designed to give man the clue, the rest were purposely left blank to encourage his skill and resource.

Introduction

It is no wonder that Ray revolted against such extravagances and dismissed all such signatures with the remark, "All that I find mentioned and collected by authors, seem to me rather fancied by men, than designed by nature". But it is worth noting that what he rejected was the evidence to support this particular example of God's concern with man's welfare, and not at all the general assumption that such a concern was to be taken for granted. Hence it is that on the same page where he dismissed signatures as merely "fancied by men", he accepts as confirmed by evidence another doctrine which seems to us quite as far-fetched.

"One observation I shall add relating to the virtues of plants, in which I think there is something of truth, that is that there are, by the wise disposition of Providence, such species of plants produced in every country as are most proper and convenient for the meat and medicine of the men and animals that are bred and inhabit there. Insomuch that Solenander writes that from the frequency of the plants that spring up naturally in any region he could easily gather what endemical diseases the inhabitants thereof were subject to."

Thus even Ray, pioneer scientist though he was, reminds us how reluctant many were to exchange a man- and God-centered universe and to take the road which has, though perhaps unnecessarily, led to that alienation which has become in modern literature and philosophy a theme almost as near the center of the writer's concern as was the medieval conviction that, however great the threats with which human life and the human soul were surrounded, God had provided all that was needful for an escape from them—the Church for a remedy against spiritual diseases, the wonderful world of plants to correct those merely physical.

HERBS AND ASTROLOGY

It is not always easy to draw a clear line between a mere superstition on the one hand and an erroneous hypothesis on the other, but there is rather more of the erroneous hypothesis in the Doctrine of Signatures and rather more of mere superstition in that mingling of medical botany with astrology which medieval devotion to the latter pseudo-science made almost inevitable. The anonymous fifteenth-century German Herbalist from whom our opening quotation was taken implies a connection when he writes how often he has "contemplated inwardly the wondrous works of the Creator of the universe: How in the beginning He formed the Heavens and adorned them with goodly, shining stars, to which He gave power and might to influence everything under Heaven. . . . Thereupon I thought on the wondrous order which the Creator gave these same creatures of His, so that everything which has its being under Heaven receives it from the stars, and keeps it by their health".

It seems that it was Paracelsus in the century following who was chiefly responsible for the extravagant elaboration of a general notion that herbs, like everything else under the sun, were to some extent influenced by the planets. He held that there was some mystical identity between each plant and the planet or star of which it was an earthly representative. Nevertheless, in England at least, it was not until the seventeenth century that astrology began to assume a very prominent place in certain Herbals, and it had its most notorious exploiter in Nathaniel Culpeper, one of the most popular of all forerunners of medical fanaticism or charlatanry. He carried on a feud with the medical establishment of his day much like that which still rages from time to time between official medicine and the proponents of cure-all health foods, folk remedies, et cetera.

Culpeper set up in London about the middle of the seventeenth century as astrologer and physician. He assigned every plant to the influence of a planet and also of a Zodiacal constellation, after which he was free to practice a very conveniently loose logic of which the following is a typical example: "Wormwood is an herb of Mars . . . I prove it thus: What delights in martial places is a martial herb; wormwood delights in martial places—for about forges and ironworks you may gather a cartload of it, ergo, it is a Martial herb." Since each illness is caused by the influence of a planet it can be cured by the use of an herb belonging to an opposing planet. Thus, diseases produced by Jupiter are healed by the herbs of Mercury. On the other hand, the illness may be cured by sympathy instead, which means by herbs belonging to the planet which caused the disorder. "Wormwood is good for afflictions of the eyes because the eyes are under the luminaries; the right eye of a man and the left eye of a woman the Sun claims dominion over: the left eye of a man and the right eye of a woman are the privilege of the Moon. Wormwood, an herb of Mars, cures both what belongs to the Sun by sympathy, because he is exalted in his house; but what belongs to the Moon by antipathy, because he hath his fall in hers."

Introduction

Even in his own time Culpeper was severely criticized for such nonsense by more respectable writers like Coles, but it may gratify the cynical to know that, while the others are totally forgotten today except by scholars, Culpeper's Herbal ran into edition after edition, and that even today books of herbal medicine which rely heavily on astrology—and still bear his name—are on sale.

HERBS AND MODERN DRUGS

The modern pharmacist stocks a bewildering number of drugs, of which an astonishing proportion have been introduced during recent decades. One immensely important category, that of the antibiotics, derives from the fungi, a group of saprophytic plants to which Dioscorides devotes a few sentences, but to which he attributes no medical virtues whatsoever. But, though some of the modern pharmacist's other drugs are also derived from plants well known to the ancient physicians, only old-fashioned drugstores in the United States (usually in foreign quarters) stock more than a negligible number of what the Herbalists call "simples"—that is, plant leaves, or seeds, or roots, or bark which might be administered alone, though they might also serve as ingredients in prescriptions which, like Jacques's melancholy, was "compounded of many simples".

The number of such simples described by the more advanced Herbalists must be even greater than that of the drugs commonly found today on a given pharmacist's shelves. Some of them were sometimes described as specifics (i.e. certain cures) for various distresses, including that of the bite of the mad dog. Pliny devotes one section of his *Natural History* to listing the names of the various plants with all the diseases they are supposed to cure. Garlic, for instance, is good for sixty-one different disorders; Lettuce for forty-two; Hawkweed for seventeen; Cabbage for eighty-seven, and Pennyroyal for twenty-five. Moreover, there is in all the Herbals a very great deal of overlapping—the same disease can be treated by any one of a dozen or more simples.

Now, it is a general rule that when many remedies are prescribed to correct any evil—physical, mental, economic, or political—it is highly probable that none of them are very effective. The number of cures available for the common cold is sufficient to demonstrate that this rule is valid today, and were it not for stern government control it is certain that we would find advertised in the magazines and on television many sure cures for everything from cancer to this same common cold—instead of those many claims that this or that "helps to relieve the symptoms of", which now rule the airwaves. Today, scarcely less than in ancient times, men are eager to believe in whatever promises deliverance from any bodily ill, whether the savior be a new wonder drug or any one of the fads which sweep the country from time to time. A few years ago it was honey and vinegar which was being recommended as a cure-all; and in that connection it is entertaining to know that nearly two thousand years ago Dioscorides was recommending for the treatment of arthritis, epilepsy, and snakebite what he called Oxymel (literally sour honey), which his English translator calls Vinegar-Honey.

In view of all this, including the fact that most of even the sure cures of the Herbalist have disappeared from the pharmacopoeias, one inevitably asks if the whole ancient medicine, admittedly based on theoretical foundations almost entirely erroneous, was no more than a grand delusion helped along by charlatanry.

That pure charlatanry did exist—as it exists today—is obvious from the number of frauds which the serious physicians tried to expose (see, for instance, the articles on Mandrake [page 100] and Henbane [page 148]), while "nostrum", one of the words we use to indicate a fraudulent medicine, is merely Latin for "ours", in reference to the faker's claim to offer an infallible remedy known to him alone. Moreover, many herbs confidently and honestly recommended probably had no physiological effect whatever. This may have been true no more often of those that owed their reputations to some theory of signatures or planetary influence than of others to which some virtue had been ascribed on the basis of what was believed to be empirical evidence. After all, people often got well then as they often get well today without owing their recovery to the drugs they have taken—sometimes, even in spite of both drugs and doctor. We still assume too often that post hoc means propter hoc. (For an example of a marvelous cure attributed in classical times to the eating of lettuce, see page 38.) And the wry joke that patients sometimes get well in spite of doctors goes back at least to an Anglo-Saxon translation, made about the year 1000, of the Herbal known as the Pseudo-Apuleius.

The fact remains, nevertheless, that the Herbalist did employ a considerable number of plants whose physiological effects were genuine, are still recognized, and, in some cases, are still commonly prescribed. He had cathartics and purges, anodynes and narcotics, vermifuges,

Introduction

emetics, carminatives, suderifics, diuretics, a heart stimulant (Helle-bore), mild digestive stimulants, counter-irritants, an antispasmodic (Licorice Root), emollients, and a number of pleasant aromatics which certainly quieted and comforted the patient even though they had no strong physiological effect. Where no effective remedy was known, it was doubtless just as well that bland, innocuous herbs were administered. They served as placebos and by inspiring hope in the patient helped to cure him.

Unfortunately, on the other hand, a few of the most effective vegetable drugs—notably Quinine and Cascara—did not reach Europe until the age of the Herbalist was drawing to a close. Even more unfortunately still, and despite the fact that these Herbalists did recognize the usefulness of a number of plants whose active principles are still employed, there were also cases where they failed to recognize extremely important drugs.

Of this, perhaps the most striking case is that of Foxglove, or Digitalis. Several species of the plant were native to Europe and Asia and it was known to both gardeners and Herbalists. In fact, it was actually administered for various purposes. But its specific effect upon the heart was not generally recognized until the late eighteenth century, when it was discovered by a Doctor William Withering in a manner which demonstrates that folk medicine sometimes has things to teach science, and which serves at the same time to illustrate how controlled observation as opposed to loose empiricism was about to transform medicine.

Doctor Withering had heard of a secret remedy for dropsy dispensed by an old woman in Shropshire and said to have sometimes affected cures where physicians had failed. Somehow (some accounts say by purchase for a large sum), he obtained the complicated recipe and guessed correctly that Foxglove was the effective ingredient. He did not know that one kind of dropsy was caused by a malfunctioning of the heart, another by a kidney disorder, but he experimented with Foxglove (or Digitalis) on a large number of patients and, though it proved to be (as it still is) a dangerous drug if not carefully measured and watched, he was ready in 1785 to publish his classic *An Account of the Foxglove and Some of its Medical Uses; With Practical Remarks on Dropsy and Other Diseases*. Thus herb medicine linked with modern research.

Interest in drugs of plant origin tended to fall sharply about the beginning of our century and then to rise sharply again in recent decades.

JWK

Around the year 1900 the major contents of the pharmacopoeias and formularies consisted of descriptive standards for crude drugs or, as the Herbalist would have called them, simples. Most of them have since almost completely disappeared, though in a number of cases their "active principles" extracted by modern chemical methods are still of major importance—as is notably the case of Digitalis, Cocaine, Quinine, Caffeine, Codeine, Resperine, Ergotine, etc.

Until his recent death, a Mexican druggist in Tucson, Arizona, boasted that he stocked more than two hundred Mexican drugs, but they were chiefly for his Latin customers, and only old-fashioned American druggists have now much call for the dried Raspberries or Catnip which some of them still stock for home preparation of suderific teas. An exception is Larkspur, which still is (or at least was until very recently) employed to kill head lice.

It was the rise of chemotherapy which put into temporary eclipse medical interest in drugs of plant origin. First Salvarsan and then the Sulpha drugs seemed to suggest that the laboratory rather than the fields and woods was the place to search for remedies against human ills. For our cures we were now to look to man's ingenuity rather than to God's goodness. Even the advertisers of proprietary remedies illustrate the extent to which the popular mind transferred its old faith in nature to the laboratory. Instead of old family remedies, Indian snakeroot and so forth, we were offered "wonder drugs", and the pictures of white-coated technicians took the place of village wise women or old family nurses.

The public has hardly yet become aware of the new turn which took place quite recently, when the effectiveness of the active principle of various old-fashioned medical herbs (many of them having figured for centuries in folk medicine) was rediscovered and when new ones were found for the first time. In certain cases, botanical medicine and chemotherapy have joined hands, for example when practitioners of the latter discovered that a compound synthesized by some plant is, rather than any inorganic substance, the best starting point for the further synthesis of a hitherto nonexistent chemical entity of possibly great medical use. For all these reasons, a new era of plant hunting has begun—and there are certainly more collectors out gathering specimens to be analyzed and tested in laboratories than there were even in the great eighteenth and nineteenth century era of botanical exploration. Some successes in this quest have been impressive.

JOSEPH WOOD KRUTCH

Introduction

The ancient physicians knew that certain plants had the power of inducing visions (see, for example, the commentary on Thorn Apple on page 218). But, except in the case of Opium and its derivatives, moderns paid little attention to this phenomenon until recently, when the active principle of both the Peyote Cactus and of certain fungi captured the imagination of both researchers and the general public by their extraordinary psychic effects.

Equally sensational and possibly more important was the discovery of the tranquilizers, derived from a member of that Dogbane family which includes the familiar Oleander. The value of this plant had been recognized for centuries both in Africa where it was given to emotionally disturbed patients and in India where it was used, not only in the treatment of insanity, but also for its tranquilizing effect upon both infants and adults (Mohammed Ghandi frequently drank a tea made from the roots of Rauwolfia, the plant in question). And yet, as the biochemist Robert de Ropp wrote:

"It is curious that a remedy so ancient . . . should have been ignored by Western researchers until the year 1947. This situation results in part, at least, from the rather contemptuous attitude which certain chemists and pharmacologists in the West have developed toward folk remedies and drugs of plant origin. . . . They further fell into the error of supposing that because they had learned the trick of synthesizing certain substances, they were better chemists than Mother Nature who, besides creating compounds too numerous to mention, also synthesized the aforesaid chemists and pharmacologists."

As a Sudanese psychiatrist connected with the World Health Organization recently advised his colleagues: "Always stay on good terms with the local witch doctor. I have learned a lot from medicine men."—a bit of advice which the story of the discovery of Digitalis tends to substantiate. The importance of Rauwolfia as well as other recently introduced or reintroduced drugs of vegetable origin suggest also that we may be entering an age during which the plant world may again supply the physician with his most useful remedies.

The story of the tranquilizers is relevant to an understanding of herbal medicine because it illustrates a phenomenon common in the history of science in general, as well as in that of medicine in particular. Erroneous hypotheses do not necessarily invalidate empirically discovered truths and may, as working hypotheses, actually lead to these truths. Thus, Ptolemaic astronomy enabled its adepts to predict eclipses and other celestial phenomena with surprising accuracy despite the fact that it was completely erroneous. Similarly, the Hindu physicians were wrong in attributing the effect of Rauwolfia to the moon, but right in describing that effect.

Perhaps the most striking case of an important medical discovery directly traceable to reliance upon a false hypothesis involves the assumption that where a malady is usually prevalent, God had placed the appropriate healing herb.

In 1763, the Reverend Edward Stone noticed that willows were likely to flourish in marshy regions where rheumatism was very common. Acting in accord with what was by then a pretty old-fashioned theory, he tried a decoction of willow bark on sufferers from rheumatism, and thus discovered the effectiveness of salicylic acid for the relief of rheumatic pains. (*Salix* is Latin for willow.) The acid was synthesized some three quarters of a century later. Not long after that, an experimentally-inclined chemist made a derivative whose superiority to salicylic acid was not recognized until later still, when it became famous under the name of aspirin. Thus we owe what modern doctors regard as one of the most useful of all drugs to what seems to us a preposterously naive theory, and if the Reverend Stone had not been rather old-fashioned in his mental attitudes we might still (who knows?) be without aspirin.

HERBALS, BOTANY, AND GARDENING

Utilitarian though they were in original intention, the Herbals gave birth not only to the useful sciences of medicine and pharmacology, but also to horticulture and to systematic botany—to the latter because classification was obviously necessary if one Herbalist was to know what another was talking about; to horticulture because he was often also a cultivator of the simples which, as physician, he prescribed.

So far as botany in general as distinguished from purely medical botany is concerned, the Herbalist naturally again looked back to the classical age for guidance. The earliest surviving Greek work on any aspect of plant science is the *History of Plants*, which appears to be based on the lecture notes taken by some pupil of Theophrastus, who had himself been a student of Aristotle and later his successor as head of the Lyceum. Though it contains a good deal of miscellaneous information, it is primarily concerned with theoretical generalizations rather

Introduction

than with medicine or the classification of individual plants. It was far less important to the Herbalists than either the writings of the Greek physician Dioscorides, who flourished during the reign of Nero, or those of Pliny the Elder, who also wrote during the first century A.D. The latter was an industrious but wholly uncritical compiler, whose *Natural History* summarizes everything he could find in existing works concerning plants, animals, and minerals. His work is also a great repository of superstitions and tall tales, which it passed on to later times —generating a good deal of that Unnatural History which the Middle Ages cherished and elaborated.

Dioscorides, on the other hand, was apparently a practicing physician. His work, which survives as a Byzantine manuscript written in the early sixth century A.D., describes hundreds of plants, mostly of the Mediterranean region, together with their use in medicine. To the Dark and the early Middle Ages he was The Master of Those Who Know, so far as plants and their uses were concerned. As in the case of such other classical authorities as were then known, the tendency was to follow him slavishly—even to the point of assuming that any plant growing in whatever region an Herbalist might live must of necessity be one of those described by Dioscorides. Moreover, the tendency of those who tried to preserve something of ancient learning as barbarism advanced was to simplify, to summarize, and to place larger and larger emphasis on the fabulous, until Dioscorides' substantial and largely rational work became some such pathetic compilation as that anonymous treatise, the tenth-century Pseudo-Apuleius. Here, beside a very crude illustration of the plant being described, is frequently placed the picture of some beast—presumably meant to inform the illiterate which herb is to be used against injury from this or that animal.

Gradually, however, as the Dark Ages gave way to the medieval and the medieval to the Renaissance, the European Herbal became more ambitious, more original, and wider in scope. At the same time, increasing attempts were made to distinguish species and to record accurately the flora of a given region. The Herbal printed in 1530 by the German Otto Brunfels is often singled out as marking the beginning of a new era, while the Anglican clergyman William Turner, who published the first part of his *New Herbal* in 1551, is often called the Father of English Botany.

The *Commentaries on the Six Books of Dioscorides,* written by the Italian Mattioli and first published in 1544, represents, despite the modesty of its title, a great advance over Dioscorides in the number of plants treated and in the great attention paid to the identification of the different species.

It is usual to regard the publication of Linnaeus' *Systema Naturae* (1735) as marking the end of the age of the Herbalists and the beginning of modern botany. Nevertheless, and in England as well as elsewhere, the gradual transformation of the Herbal into books concerned with plants interesting scientifically or esthetically as well as medically had been going on since about the end of the sixteenth century. Gerard's *The Herbal, or General History of Plants* (1597) is not by any means exclusively medical; Parkinson's *Paradisi in Sole Paradisus Terrestris; A Garden of All Sorts of Pleasant Flowers Which Our English Ayre Will Permit to be Noursed Up* (1629) is not even largely such. Culpeper's *The English Physician Enlarged* (1653) and Coles' *The Art of Simpling* (1656) are, on the other hand, more in the nature of old-fashioned Herbals, while John Evelyn's *Kalendarium Hortense* (1664) which is, despite its title, written in English, is probably the first of the Garden Calendars addressed entirely to those interested in what were called "gardens of delight" as opposed to herb or medical gardens.

HERBS IN COOKERY

Though the culinary use of herbs is probably as old or older than their use in medicine, much less writing about it survives from classical times —partly, perhaps, because the Greeks would have classified cooking among the "mechanical" arts and therefore unworthy of the attention of those entitled to a "liberal" education. There is, on the other hand, abundant evidence that in the medieval kitchen herbs were at least as important as they are in to-day's haute cuisine. Their twofold importance is neatly recognized in the medieval story which tells how, when the scholar Alcuin asked his pupil Charlemagne "What is an herb?", the Emperor replied, "The friend of physicians and the praise of cooks".

Two fourteenth-century books, the English *Form of Curry* [Cookery] and the French *Le Ménager de Paris,* contain elaborate recipes that take for granted all the herbs now commonly used, as well as some that have pretty well disappeared from the kitchen. Among those which *Le Ménager de Paris* calls for are: Anise, Basil, Bay, Borage, Caraway, Salvia, Coriander, Dill, Fennel, Marjoram, Mint, Parsley, Sage, and many others. Many of these same herbs had appeared nearly four hun-

Introduction

dred years earlier in a list of more than seventy herbs and vegetables which Charlemagne directed his subjects to cultivate in their gardens, and they had probably been in use since the dawn of history.

Throughout the Middle Ages, an herb and kitchen garden—often including ornamentals also—was an expected feature of every monastery. Then, as times grew less hard and the Renaissance spread from Italy throughout Europe, all kinds of gardens grew more elaborate. In England, Shakespeare's contemporary, John Parkinson, tended gardens in which he grew not only all the usual herbs important in medicine or cookery, but also many curiosities including Tomatoes, Potatoes, Tobacco, and Nasturtiums from the New World, Tiger Lilies from Constantinople, and Ginger (which winter killed) from Barbary.

Perhaps the best straightforward description of a "Garden of Delight" in Shakespeare's day is from a book of instruction by the journalist Gervaise Markham:

"The Garden of Pleasure shall be set about and compassed with arbors made of jessamin, rosemarie, box, juniper, cypress-trees, savin, cedars, rose-trees and other dainties first planted and pruned . . .

"This garden, by means of a large path of the breadth of six feet, shall be divided into two equal parts; the one shall contain the herbs and flowers used to make nosegays and garlands of, as March violets, Provence gilliflowers, purple gilliflowers, Indian gilliflowers, small pansies, daisies, yellow and white gilliflowers, marigolds, lily connally, daffodills, Canterbury bells, purple velvet flowers, anemones, corn-flag, mugwort, lilies and other such-like; and it may be indeed the Nosegay Garden.

"The other part shall have all other sweet-smelling herbs whether they be such as bear no flowers, or, if they bear any, yet they are not put in nosegays alone, but the whole herb with them, as Southernwood, wormwood, pellitory, rosemary, jessamine, marjerom, balm-mints, pennyroyal, costmarie, hyssop, lavander, basil, sage, savory, rue, tansey, thyme, camomile, mugwort, bastard marjerom, nept, sweet balm, all-good, anis, horehound and other such like; and this may be called the garden for herbs and good smell."

The earliest American colonists learned from the Indians to use certain native plants for seasoning, but they were also soon importing a great variety of seeds from the old country. As early as 1738 a newspaper advertisement offered as "just arrived from London" Anise, Caraway,

34

and Fennel seeds. Later in the same century another newspaper announcement describes as "lately imported from Italy" Sweet Basil, Chevril, and Poppy. By the beginning of the nineteenth century, the Philadelphia nursery of the famous Bartrams, father and son, was supplying many different herbs and, because interest in herb cookery has greatly increased in recent years, there are to-day many commercial suppliers both large and small.

The present volume aims simply to entertain (and perhaps inform) those who share the author's interest in the facts and fancies which constituted our forefathers' knowledge of the world of plants, and who find in it a charm for which the grimmer science of our own day offers no equivalent.

The ancient Herbals vary enormously in the number and identity of the species included. The one hundred chosen for treatment here were selected largely on the basis of the number of interesting things which had been or could be said about them, and the attractiveness of the plates. In other ways also, the plan of the book is as informal as possible. It pretends to no sort of completeness or logical order, either as a whole or in respect to the individual commentaries. If it had a model it was, perhaps, the work of that garrulous, gossipy compiler, Pliny the Elder.

Closely regarded, every one of the individual plants will be found useful, beautiful, or wonderful—and not infrequently all three. Perhaps the chief charm of the Herbalists (and certainly the one this book would like especially to suggest) is just that they are more likely than the modern scientist to impart a sense of beauty and wonder—both of which the scientist may feel, but considers it no part of his function to communicate.

THE PLATES

See the Bibliography (page 249) for brief notes on the authors and
books most frequently cited in the texts which follow.

Bog Asphodel

FOR MORE *than two thousand years the Asphodel has been a great favorite of the poets from Homer (who makes it flourish in the Elysian Fields) to Tennyson (whose Lotus eaters dwell in Elysian valleys "Resting weary limbs at last on beds of Asphodel").*

Unfortunately, even the best poets are not always expert in taxonomy and their Asphodel seems to be sometimes what we call a Narcissus, sometimes a Daffodil, and sometimes still another member of the Lily family.

So far as Mattioli is concerned, it is evident from the illustration that his Asphodelus is one of the Bog or Bastard Asphodels, certain species of which are native to the Mediterranean region, and at least two to North America. All belong to the Lily family, but the Bog Asphodel is put in a genus of its own and given the name Narthecium. *The American species are* N. americanum *and* N. califirnicum.

"Daffodil" is, by the way, merely a corruption of "Asphodel", and a good illustration of the fact that a Rose by any other name would not necessarily smell as sweet in verse. If Tennyson's Asphodel has an aura of the classics, Wordsworth's Daffodil is homely and English.

Pliny, speaking perhaps of the true rather than the Bog Asphodel, lists fifty-one disorders which it will cure; quotes Hesiod as saying that it will protect against evil spirits; and adds that it will also exterminate or drive away rats if placed in front of their holes.

Mattioli, also following Dioscorides and other ancient authorities, attributes a great many medicinal virtues to the Asphodel. The roots, he says, are piquant and a beverage made from them will provoke urination and the menstrual flow. With wine they cure hernias, spasms and coughs. Mashed, these same roots protect against snake bite and if mixed with flowers and leaves should be applied to ulcers and inflamed breasts or testicles. Juice of the root boiled with Myrrh is singularly good for the eyes. Reduced to ashes it causes hair to grow. To cure a toothache, this same mixture should be poured into the ear on the opposite side of the head from the offending tooth. And finally, Crateus, an ancient Herbalist, is responsible for the statement that "the root being drunk makes men to have no appetite to venery".

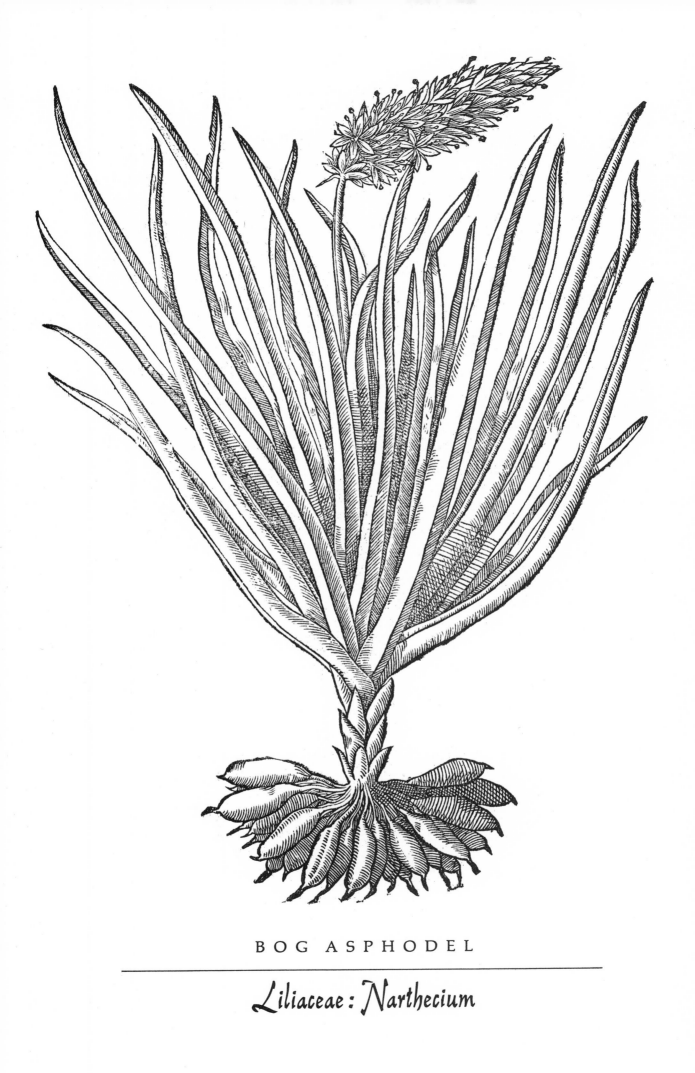

BOG ASPHODEL

Liliaceae : Narthecium

Lettuce

THE PER CAPITA *consumption of Lettuce was certainly never greater than it is today and neither was its somewhat vague reputation of being "good for you". Nevertheless, it was a favorite vegetable with the ancients also and credited with astonishing medicinal virtues. Pliny tells the following story vouched for by other early writers:*

"We find it stated that the late Emperor Augustus when ill was saved on one occasion, thanks to the skill of his physician Musa, by eating Lettuce, a food which the excessive scruples of his former physician had forbidden him. At the present day, however, Lettuces have risen into such high esteem that a method has been discovered of preserving them even during the months when they are out of season by keeping them in Oxymel [i.e. honey and vinegar mixed]."

It is also reported that for having saved the life of Augustus, Musa was rewarded by a large sum of money, permission to wear a gold ring, and by the erection by public subscription of a statue in his honor not far from that of Aesculapius. (Musa was probably neither the first nor the last physician to acknowledge gratitude for a remarkable cure while wondering privately just how this patient happened to get well.)

Mattioli devotes a long chapter to the reputation of Lettuce as a remedy for a wide variety of diseases. The oddest recommendation is that it be mixed with woman's milk and applied to soothe burns. Galen says that when he was young, he was much troubled with bile in the stomach, which was relieved by eating Lettuce. "Being now old and desiring nothing except repose, the same food gives me great help. I had so accustomed myself in youth to stay awake and study that in age I was much irritated by inability to sleep. Against this annoyance I have found no better remedy than eating Lettuce in the evening."

In view of the American habit (especially in restaurants) of serving a salad first, the following epigram by Martial is interesting:

"In the good old days they used to put Lettuce on the table at dessert time. Tell me, then, why now-a-days it's the first thing served?"

Most of the garden kinds such as Head Lettuce, Curled Lettuce, Romaine, etc., are all varieties of the botanical species Lactuca sativa *and probably all cultigens—that is, vegetable forms which originated in cultivation.*

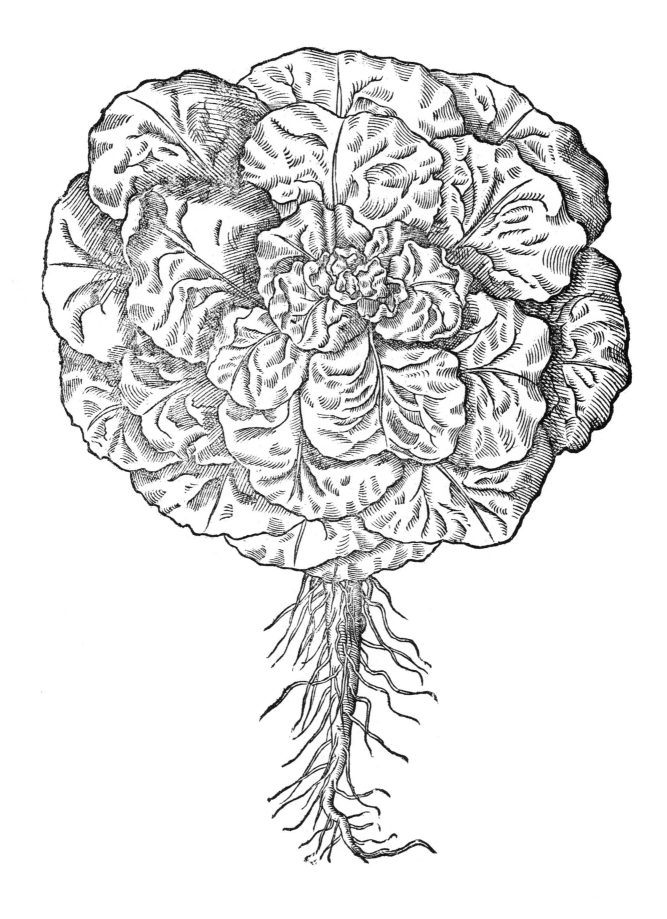

LETTUCE

Compositae: Lactuca

Cumin

CUMIN *is known today chiefly as one of the essential ingredients of curry powder; as the dominant flavor in kummel; and as a flavoring in sauerkraut as well as in some German breadstuffs. Like Anise, Coriander, and Dill, it belongs to the Carrot family and it was once much more prominent in the medicine chest and the kitchen than it is today. Both the Old and New Testaments, the writings attributed to Hippocrites, and the works of Galen make mention of it. In medieval cookery, it was a favorite seasoning for fowl, including peacock, and it was essential in an imposing dish called "Comminée de Poulaille", which consisted of chicken cooked in wine, then fried, then cut into small pieces with Ginger, Saffron, and Cumin.*

The Herbalists sometimes distinguished between the wild sort and that grown in gardens but there was probably no specific difference between the two. "Its virtue", says Banckes' Herbal, "is to destroy wicked winds and other evils in a man's stomach" and that statement still holds good. The ancient writers usually, however, attributed to it more sensational characteristics and surrounded it with certain superstitions, notably the belief, reported by Theophrastus, that you must curse the seed when sowing if you want a good crop.

Dioscorides says that "it changeth also the skin into a paler color being either drank or smeared on", and in connection with that fact or alleged fact, Pliney tells one of his more amusing anecdotes:

"It is generally stated that the disciples of Porcius Latro, so celebrated among the professors of eloquence, used to employ this drink for the purpose of imitating the paleness which had been contracted by their master through the intensities of his studies; and that Julius Vindex [the leader of a revolt against Nero] in more recent times adopted this method of playing upon those who were looking for a place in his will." (i.e. In order, like Ben Jonson's Volpone, to encourage the hopeful to curry favor by bringing him gifts in anticipation of his proximate demise.)

Gerard reports: "I have proved the seeds in my garden where they have brought forth ripe seed much fairer and greater than any that comes from beyond the seas."

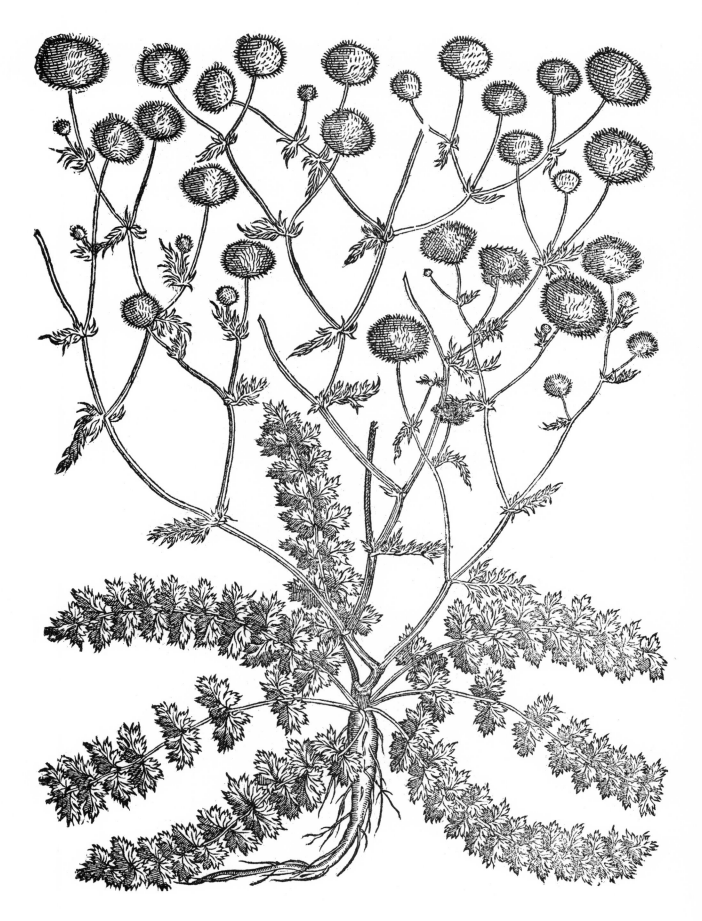

CUMIN

Umbelliferae : Cumin

Arum

TO AMERICANS, *the most familiar names for any of the wild Arums are Jack-in-the-pulpit for one sort and Skunk Cabbage for another; but there are various other colloquial names in English, notably Lords-and-Ladies, Cuckoopint, and Wake-Robin.*

No "signature" is more immodestly evident than that provided by the very phallic central column (actually a spadix bearing the small male and female flowers) and most of the popular names embody evidence, now somewhat obscured, that the folk imagination had deciphered the signature. Cuckoopint is short for Cuckoopintel, and Wake-Robin (though now gently poetic) was clear enough to those same Elizabethans who snickered when the mad Ophelia sang "For bonnie sweet Robin is all my joy".

Probably because the Doctrine of Signatures was not attended to in classical times, it is the later Herbalists who stress the supposed effectiveness of the Arums as aphrodisiacs. Dioscorides treats four species, but to him certain medical virtues and the fact that the corm supplies a starch useful in the laundry as well as for food are the important facts. Here, on the contrary, is what Coles has to say of the Cuckoopint:

"It hath not only the signature which will sufficiently declare itself but the virtues also according to the signature, for they are notable for stirring up of inclination to copulation, being either well roasted under the embers or boiled." He then adds that among other names are Sacerdotis Penis, or, in English, Priests Pintle.

The generally outré appearance of the Arums no doubt encouraged superstitions of all sorts and Gerard blames the following bit of picturesque nonsense on the most revered ancient authorities:

"Bears, after they have lain in their den four days without any manner of sustenance but what they got with licking and sucking their own feet do, as soon as they come forth, eat the herb Cuckoopint; through the windy nature thereof the hungry gut is opened and made fit again to receive sustenance, for by abstaining from food so long a time the gut is shrunk or drawn so close together that in a manner it is quite shut up, as Aristotle, Aelianus, Plutarch, Pliny, and others do write."

ARUM

Araceae : Arum

Crocus

ALL THE CROCUSES *are natives of the Mediterranean and East Asian region. One very pretty purple species is still a fairly common wild flower in Greece, but the only one of much interest to the old Herbalists or to the modern cook is the Saffron* (Crocus sativa), *which probably originated in the Near East but has been widely cultivated in many places from classical times down to the present.*

Only the dried stigmas are used, and since it is said that four thousand are required to provide one ounce of Saffron, it may be that, like the peacock brains of the Roman epicure, Saffron was valued partly because it was so scarce and expensive. But that was by no means the only reason. It was a drug, a dye, a perfume, and a kitchen flavor.

The Herbalists were naturally most concerned with its medical virtues; with the varieties believed to be most effective; and with the detection of adulturation, which the scarcity of the genuine made very tempting. Despite their assurance that it was good for a wide variety of disorders and could also be made to serve such dubious purposes as inhibiting intoxication and "provoking luxury", Saffron has now all but disappeared from medicine while holding its place in the kitchen. There it figures importantly in many dishes, especially those which involve Spanish rice. As a perfume, Saffron is mentioned in the Song of Solomon *and is one of the ingredients in the dye used to make the spot on the forehead of the Hindu pundit.*

In ancient Greece, cloth dyed with Saffron was considered appropriate for royal robes and for women of the court, although, by a familiar cultural process, it later became the distinctive badge of the hetairai. As a flavoring, it was so popular in the Middle Ages that it is said to be called for in nearly a third of all the recipes which have come down to us, and one emotional forerunner of Fanny Farmer writes thus: "For hen in broth, color it with Saffron for God's sake". Henry VIII was so fond of it in his food that he is said to have prohibited court ladies from using it as a hair dye; also to have forbade the dyeing of Irish linen with Saffron because, so he feared, such colored linen would not be washed often enough.

The Saffron Crocus blooms in the autumn, but must not be confused with what is commonly called the Autumn Crocus—which isn't a Crocus at all but a Lily.

CROCUS

Iridaceae : Crocus

Banana [plant]

WE DON'T *often remember that the humble Banana, now in dependable supply in every supermarket, was once—and not so long ago —a rare and dazzling exotic, usually brought from "the Indies". It was so representative of that supposed Eden that the specific name given to one variety was* Paradisiaca. *Modern botanists believe that its original homeland was Asia; that it had been cultivated there for a very long time; that it was introduced somehow into the Western Hemisphere and then brought into Europe by early explorers of the New World.*

Dioscorides does not mention it and it is evident that Mattioli knew it from hearsay only. He puts it among the Palms (where it most decidedly does not belong) and writes as follows: "There are a good many who place among the Palms a plant which grows in Egypt and in Cyprus that the Venetians call Musa. This plant (according to those who have seen it in these countries) is five or six cubits high and is planted as other sprouts are. . . . It has no branches and is trunk only. The fruits . . . are about the size of a small cucumber and turn yellow at maturity. It is peeled before being eaten."

At about the same time that Mattioli was publishing this description, one John White was bringing back to England the earliest known drawings of the inhabitants, the flora, and the fauna of the New World. Among them was an excellent picture of what he calls the "Plantano", that name being one which still survives as Plantain and is applied to one of the less sweet members of the genus Musa. White was one of twelve settlers dispatched to Roanoke by Sir Walter Raleigh in 1585 and, although we know little more about him, twenty-three of his drawings appeared in Hakluyt's Voyages, *while fifty-two more (including that of the Plantano) turned up nearly two centuries later in the British Museum.*

Both the Musa of Mattioli and the Plantano of White are cultivated plants and sufficiently different from any known wild relative to make it evident that they are the result of many centuries of selection, in the course of which the fruit became larger, sweeter, and seedless. A number of different species or varieties are now cultivated, the most usual being Musa paradisiaca variety sapientua.

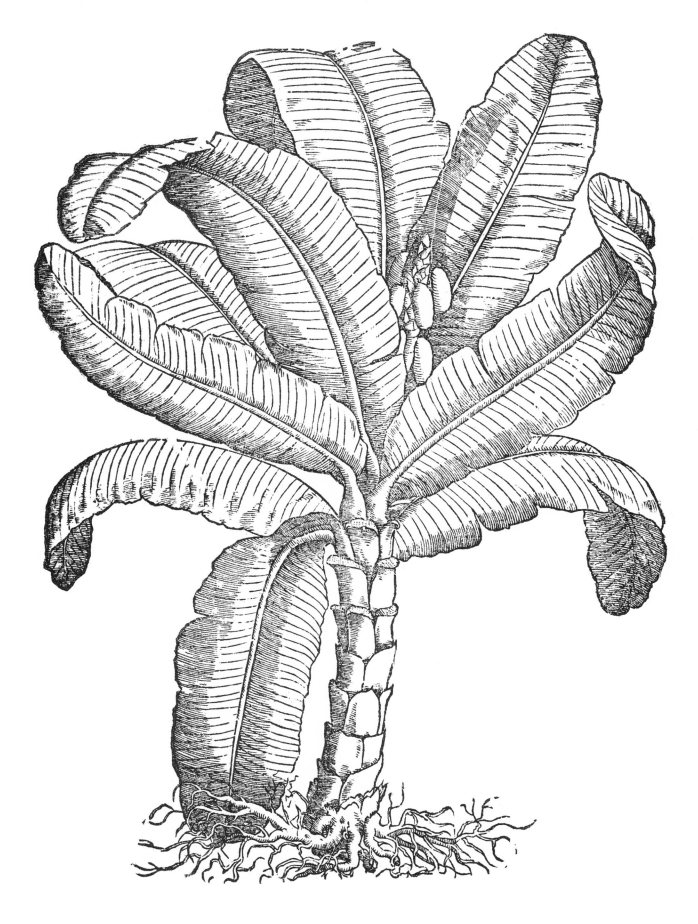

B A N A N A [Plant]

Musaceae : Musa

Banana [fruit]

WHEN MATTIOLI *published his second-hand account of the Banana, the great age of plant exploration and propagation was about to begin. Only a few years later, John Gerard, London surgeon and horticulturist, published a list of the more than one-thousand species he had grown in his London garden, and in 1597 re-issued the first edition of his famous Herbal. It was to be reprinted again and again in the seventeenth century with many revisions and additions.*

One of the later editions includes the account of a successful attempt to ripen Bananas in London. Between the lines one may recognize the change coming over the Herbalists, in whom the merely utilitarian spirit of the older botanists was giving way to the scientific and esthetic interests of a new generation of gardeners.

On April 10, 1633, Dr. Argent (later president of the College of Physicians and Surgeons of London) gave Gerard a Banana plant which Dr. Argent had received from the Bermudas. The fruit was about five inches long and not yet ripe, but when hung indoors it ripened by March and lasted until June. "The pulp or meat was very soft and tender and it did eat somewhat like a Muskmelon . . . I could observe no seed in the fruit. . . . This plant is found in many places of Asia, Africa and America especially in hot regions. You may find frequent mentions of it amongst sea voyages to East and West Indies, by the name of Plantaines, Plantanus, Bananas, etc. Some have judged it the forbidden fruit; others the Grapes brought to Moses out of the Holy Land."

All the early describers of the Banana were puzzled by the absence of seeds (actually the result of artificial selection practiced by growers in its native countries) and by the fact that the plant itself is large like a tree but soft like an herb—which last it is by modern botanical definition. The greatest mistake of the Gerard Herbal is the statement that the fruit affords little nourishment. These early students would have been astonished to know that at the very moment when they were thus dismissing it, the Banana was supplying millions of people with their principal food. They would have been even more astonished could they have known that some sixty million bunches are now said to be imported annually into the United States and that the use of the fruit in diets comes close to making it what they would have called a "simple".

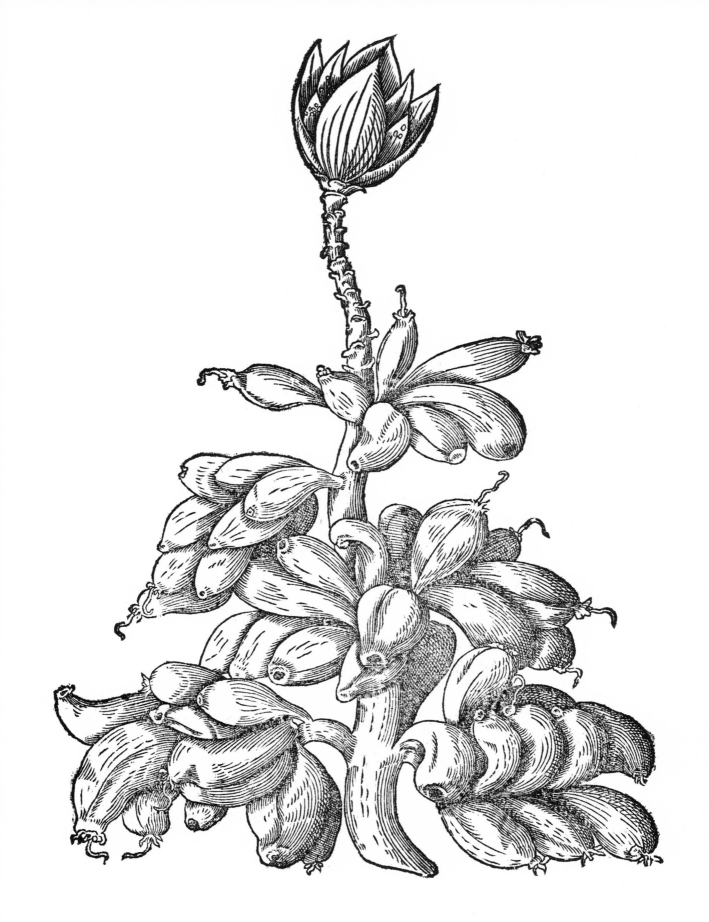

B A N A N A [Fruit]

Musaceae : Musa

Lavender

"OIL OF LAVENDER", *says Dioscorides, "when made by passing flowers through a glass alembic [i.e. when distilled] surpasses all other perfumes". And that, he says, is why grocers keep it outside of their shops: so that it will not interfere with the odors of Musk, Ambergris, Civet, and the other drugs which they stock.*

During the Middle Ages and the Renaissance, Lavender was the favorite of all scented herbs. Its Latin name Lavandula *relates to washing, in reference to its use in bath water. The medieval housewife put it in clothes chests (just as old-fashioned people still do) for the scent and to discourage insects. According to the German* Hortus Sanitatis, *the Virgin Mary was especially fond of it because it protected clothes from "dirty filthy beasts", and also preserved chastity. "If the head is sprinkled wtih Lavender water a person is chaste as long as he bears it upon him."*

Perhaps because the ancient Greeks and Romans were not very keenly interested in this particular virtue they do not seem to have discovered Lavender's ability to help in its cultivation. Dioscorides treats it very briefly, and of its utility says only: "The decoction of it is like that of Hyssop, good for griefs in the thorax. It is also mingled profitably with Antidotes." The Hortus Sanitatis, *on the other hand, credits it with remarkable effectiveness against apoplexy, palsy and loss of speech. To cure headache, Lavender should be mixed with Marjoram, Clove, Pinks, Betony, and Rose leaves and worn in a little bag around the neck. The author, apparently not a leveller, adds that for noblemen this bag should be of red silk, but that common people may use cheaper material.*

Mattioli also vouches for the medicinal virtues of Lavender. "It is much used in maladies and those disorders of the brain due to coldness, such as epilepsy, apoplexy, spasms and paralysis. It comforts the stomach, and is a great help in obstructions of the liver or spleen." Among the English Herbalists, both the sober Gerard and the extravagant Culpeper attribute to it much the same virtues. As is usual in the case of an herbal remedy which has managed to retain a foothold in modern pharmacopoeia, its "virtues" have become drastically attenuated and it is now recommended chiefly as an ingredient in Aromatic Spirits of Ammonia and perfumed soap.

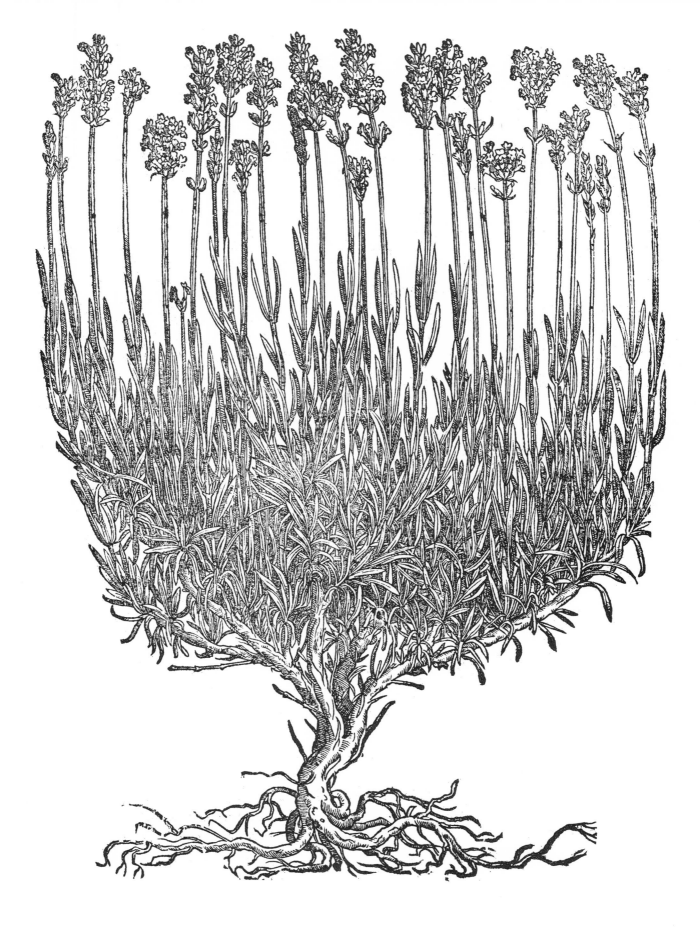

LAVENDER

Labiatae: Lavandula

Deer

ACCORDING TO ARISTOTLE, *members of the Deer family are extremely fond of music. The medieval Bestiaries not only repeat this interesting bit of information but add a good many more. If a Deer has been pierced by arrows, he may easily get rid of them by eating some Dittany and then giving himself a good shake. Moreover, as the twelfth-century manuscript translated by T. H. White has it: "These creatures are enemies to serpents. When they feel themselves to be weighed down by illness, they suck snakes from their holes with a snort of the nostrils and, the danger of their venom having been survived, the stags are restored to health by a meal of them."*

As far as medicine was concerned, the chief use of the Deer was to obtain a substance produced by burning the horns. And that is not as peculiar as may seem at first sight. Old-fashioned people still sometimes call sal volatile (smelling salts) by its old name Hartshorn, because ammonium carbonate was long prepared in just the way that Dioscorides recommends. By way of additional flourish, White's Bestiary instructs us that "the one of the horns on the right side of the head is the more useful for healing things".

DEER

Horse Chestnut

IN A CHAPTER *dealing with the true Chestnut, Mattioli writes: "Nature has also furnished us Westerners with a kind of Chestnut of which neither the ancients nor any of the moderns have, so far as I know, ever written. The tree is rather large and the leaves are divided into six parts like those of the Christ Palm [Castor Bean] . . . Its burrs come at the summit, being about the same size as ours, reddish in color, and with a tougher skin than the other kind . . . Each burr contains only one chestnut . . . It is larger and rounder." From this description it is easy to recognize the Buckeye which generations of Americans have carried in their pockets for luck. Some kinds are native in the United States, and the Old World species referred to above is widely planted here.*

It is not surprising that the ancients supposed the Buckeye to be a kind of Chestnut, since both the burrs and the nuts are strikingly similar in several respects. The leaves and flowers, on the other hand, are quite different and the two families (Fagaceae *and* Aescules) *are not even remotely related. The qualifying adjective "horse" is very commonly used in English to suggest the coarse or crude—as in Horse Radish, Horse Mint, and even horse laugh. Hence, one would naturally assume this to be the explanation of Horse Chestnut. But it is not that given by Mattioli. "In Constantinople", he says, "they are called Horse Chestnuts because if fed to broken-winded horses they will effect a cure".*

The species to which Mattioli no doubt refers is said to be native to north and central Asia and to have been introduced into England about the middle of the sixteenth century. He seems to assume that the virtues of the two Chestnuts are the same and these, if one may believe him, are sufficiently remarkable: "Chestnuts, especially if dried, effectively arrest all fluxes of the stomach and are very helpful to those who spit blood. Salted, mixed with honey, and applied to the bite of a mad dog they relieve it . . . Those which have an incision cut in the rind and then roasted in coals are the best; even better than the boiled, especially if eaten with salt, pepper or sugar."

HORSE CHESTNUT

Hippocastanaceae : Aesculus

Mistletoe

THERE ARE MANY *species of Mistletoe, all parasitic on one or more trees or shrubs. The species described by Mattioli is undoubtedly the* Viscum album *famous in European folklore. It does not grow in the United States, where we substitute for it a member of another genus of the same family,* Phoradendron flavescens.

Though none of the early botanists seem to have clearly understood parasitism, they knew that Mistletoe grew only on certain trees and that the seeds were distributed by birds. Perhaps the fact that it is obviously somehow different from other plants is responsible for the sacred-accursed status which it held. Today it is only a Christmas decoration with mildly erotic associations, but once it rivaled the Mandrake in the importance of its magical associations. Frazier thinks it was the Golden Bough which Aeneus picked to protect him during his trip to the underworld. It was the one missile capable of wounding the good Balder, and was so sacred to the Druids that, according to Julius Caesar, it was cut by white-robed priestesses with a golden sickle. After the secret of its relation to the host plant was discovered, legend said it had been degraded to parasitism because it had permitted itself to be used in the construction of the Holy Cross.

Most Herbalists make only modest claims for Mistletoe as a medicine, but The Book of Secrets, *wrongly attributed to Albertus Magnus, gives it magical properties: If you take it into your mouth and think of something you very much want to happen, it will leap out unless your hopes are going to be fulfilled. Centuries later, Culpeper is making extravagant claims. He knew of a young lady whom famous doctors had failed to cure of "falling sickness" [epilepsy] that was so severe that she had eight or ten dreadful fits a day, but was nevertheless cured "only by the powder of true Mistletoe, given, as much as would lie on a sixpence, early in the morning in black cherry water or in beer, for some days near the full moon".*

The modern common name comes through the Anglo-Saxon and was already being used by Turner. Though its origin is doubtful, it may be connected with a fact which intrigued the Herbalists: The sticky berries of a plant which depends upon birds for its propagation is used to make birdlime for capturing them. Turner quotes a Latin proverb: "Turdus ipse sibi malum cacat" [His own excrement becomes his misfortune].

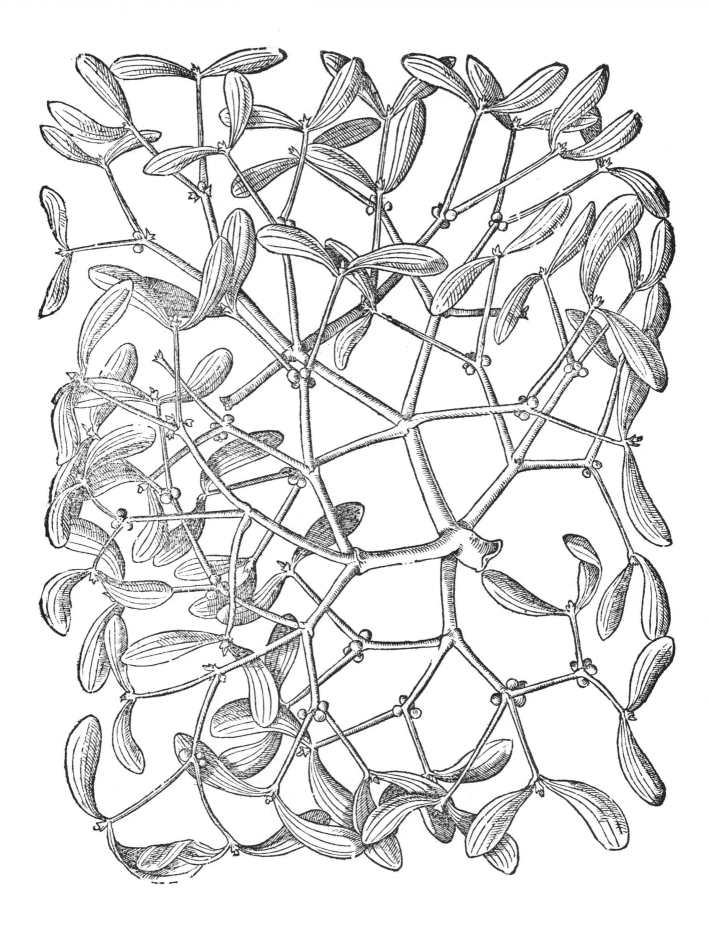

MISTLETOE

Loranthaceae : Viscum

Myrrh

THE NAME *Myrrh is derived from a Greek word meaning "perfume", and was therefore sometimes used by the Herbalists both for odoriferous gums (Frankincense and Myrrh) and for a common herb of the Carrot family which in English is called Sweet Cicely. It is not native in the United States, though we commonly call some members of the same family by the same popular name.*

Mattioli's species is the modern Myrrhis oderata, *which he believes to be that which Dioscorides says grew on Mount Ida. It is recommended, among other things, to ease the pains of parturition whether in women or in goats. According to some Herbalists it is also good for those who cannot urinate except drop by drop, and for those who can't breathe unless their head is upright. Elsewhere it has been described as a valuable tonic for girls from fifteen to eighteen, presumably for that somewhat mysterious ailment called green-sickness which, if one may judge by the numerous literary references in the writings of Shakespeare and his contemporaries, must have been very prevalent among young girls in their day. It was characterized by a sallow or greenish complexion and often by morbid appetites. "Out you green-sickness carrion, out you baggage, you tallow face", writes Shakespeare.*

Modern medicine recognizes green-sickness somewhat vaguely under the name of chlorosis (which, of course, is only a learned way of saying "greenishness") and defines it as "a form of anemia in adolescent girls, perhaps due to a faulty diet during puberty". I am not aware that Sweet Cicely is still prescribed, but in the Carrot family are various aromatic herbs including Cumin, Corriander, and Fennel, all of which are carminative, expectorant, and might increase appetite.

The translator of Dioscorides tries to avoid confusion by calling Sweet Cicely "Myrrhis" and the aromatic gum "Myrrha". The latter he describes as the tears from an Arabian tree, shed when an incision is made. Some of the exudation adheres to the trunk, some is caught on mats spread on the ground. As is usual in the case of exotic drugs, Dioscorides is concerned with distinguishing the best from inferior kinds and warning against the inevitable swindlers who palm off some sort of gum which has been macerated in water and perfumed with genuine Myrrh.

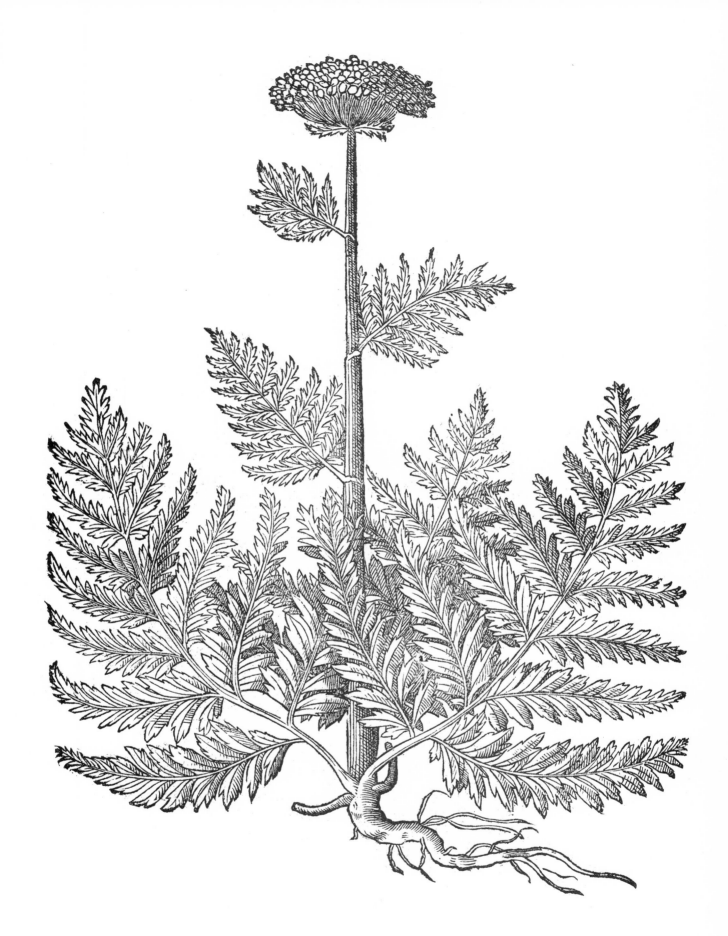

MYRRH

Umbelliferae: Myrrhis

Water Lily

THE ANCIENT (*and also the modern*) *scientific name for the Water Lily is Greek for Nymph, in obvious reference to the fact that both of these beauties preferred watery headquarters. Neither Mattioli nor his master Dioscorides seems to have been familiar with the most famous member of the family, the Egyptian Lotus, but both speak of two kinds.*

If one thinks of the whole world rather than of Europe only, there is no other flower, not even the Rose, which has been used so widely and so often as a type of the beautiful, as a decorative motif, or as a symbol of so many different things. Use of the Water Lily as a symbol apparently came rather late into Europe from Egypt and Asia. Nevertheless, the Lotus does appear as a decorative motif in classical times, and also, according to tradition, on Solomon's temple.

The Lotus which Ulysses, alone of all the heroes returning from the Trojan war, refused to eat was certainly not a Water Lily, since no member of that family could have reduced the heroes to such languor, but what the narcotic Lotus was is a difficult question. Various solutions have been proposed, the most usual being that it was the Jujube tree (see page 124), but the orientalist Sir Richard Burton favored Hashish, the Lotus of the modern Beatniks, who know it by the Mexican name Marijuana.

Most of us have heard the tale of the wheat found in an Egyptian tomb, which sprouted after thousands of years. Usually the story is told to demonstrate that life is potentially immortal, and the skeptical have always replied, "Nonsense". In the first place, there is no record of the sprouting of ancient Egyptian wheat and in the second place, though many seeds can remain dormant for a long time, they can't, it was said, possibly be still viable after hundreds, much less thousands, of years. Then, in 1923, a Japanese botanist found seeds of an extinct species of Lotus in a Manchurian bog. He planted them and they grew, although he guessed that they were some centuries old. When they were later tested by the radioactive carbon method they turned out to have been produced by a plant which had been growing at least a thousand years ago. That doesn't mean that they would have been everlasting and probably no seed is, but the experience puts the Egyptian Wheat story back into the realm of the possible, and may remind the mystical that the Lotus is the Hindu symbol of immortality.

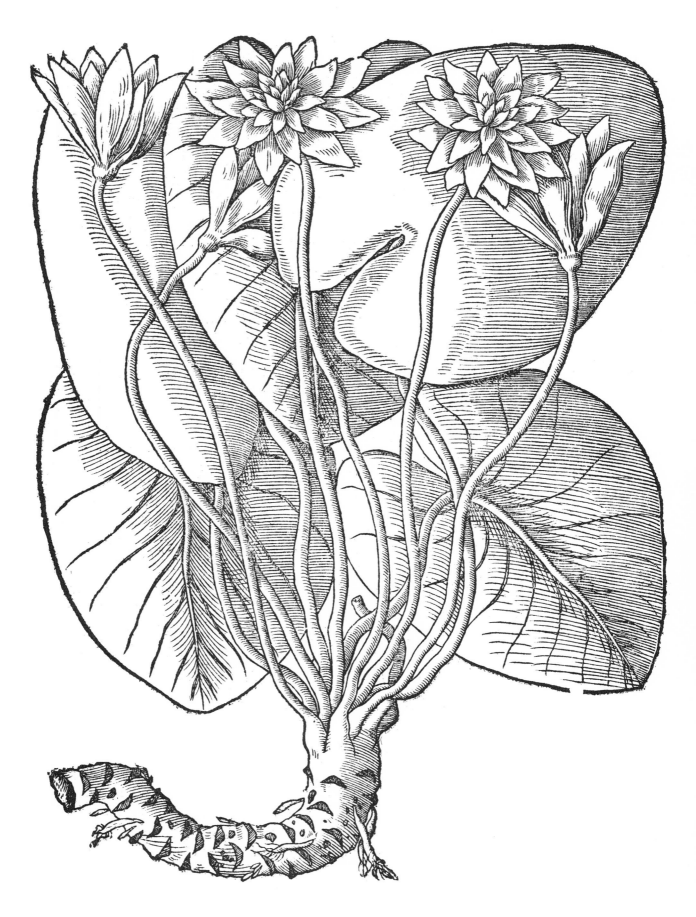

WATER LILY

Nymphaeaceae : Nymphaea

Rush

THE RUSH FAMILY *includes seven or eight genera and some two or three hundred species of grass-like plants, mostly of wet ground. In our world they are of minimal importance either for utility or ornamentation, but we are likely to forget that until quite recent times civilized man depended upon many natural products which have now been replaced by manufactured substances or articles, very much as human or animal labor has been replaced by machines. The Rushes are a striking example.*

Pliny says there are twenty-eight kinds (he appears to have confused the Rushes and other similar grass-like plants) and that they are "equally indispensable for the emergencies of war and peace". In the north they are used to make roofs which will last for centuries. "Rushes are employed, too, for writing upon paper, those of Egypt more particularly, which have a close affinity to the Papyrus." Inferior Italian species were used for tavern beds in place of feathers, and for caulking ships, while in the East they served as arrows.

A more poetic use was in the making of musical pipes, for which the Rushes growing on Lake Orchomenus (presumably near the Acadian city of the same name) were especially famous. Yet, in Pliny's time technology was already beginning to stir, and he remarks that the ancients lavished so much care on the reeds to be used for musical pipes that the modern use of silver is "excusable".

In the Middle Ages, they were used to strew on the cold stone floors and were swept away when dirty. If one may believe the story tellers, even the streets were sometimes spread with Rushes as they are in one of the narratives of the twelfth-century poet Chrétien de Troyes. One of the more attractive habits of our medieval ancestors was that of strewing about not only Rushes, but various sweet smelling herbs and flowers on floors, couches, beds, etc. In one of the songs translated by Helen Waddel in her Medieval Latin Lyrics, *a lover endeavoring to entice his lady into his room assures her that:*

> *I have made it fine for thee.*
> *Here there be couches spread,*
> *Tapestry tented,*
> *Flowers for thee to tread*
> *Green herbs, sweet scented.*

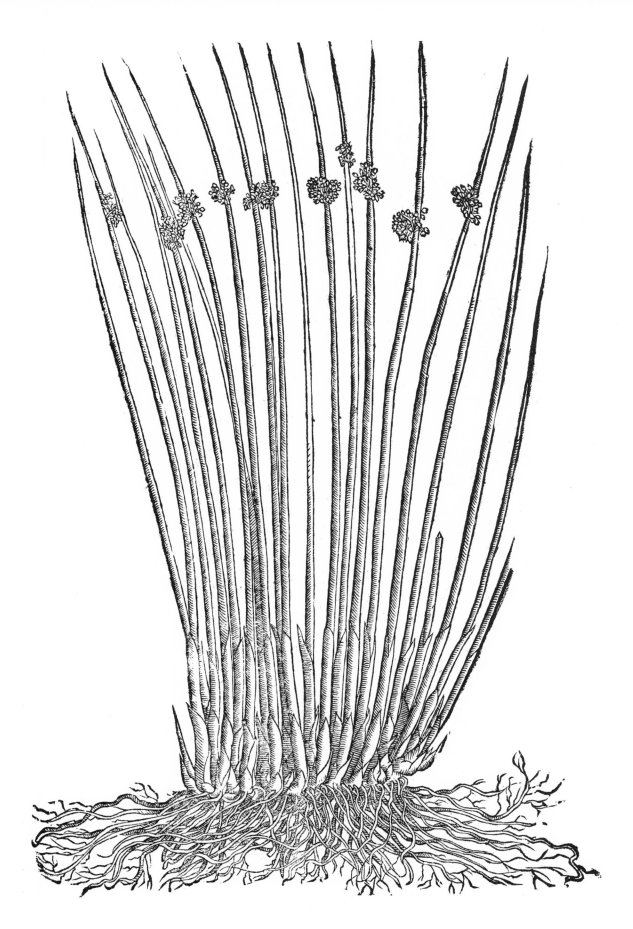

RUSH

Juncaceae : Juncus

Date Palm

TWO SPECIES *of Palm were known to ancient Greece—the Date Palm* (Phoenix dactylifera) *and a small, fan-leaved Palm of another genus. Though both remained somewhat exotic and the Date Palm would not bear fruit there, Palms appear as decorative motifs on gold cups of the Bronze Age in Greece. The trees were common in renaissance Italy in the gardens of fine houses, convents, etc., but the climate did not permit the fruit to ripen.*

Perhaps because of the Palm's beauty as well as the tremendous importance of its fruit it has been sacred in many cultures. The modern botanical name of the genus is said to be a reference to a belief that if buried to the ground it would spring up out of the ashes like "the Arabian bird of loudest lay". Theseus is said to have broken branches from the Date Palm to celebrate his victory over the Minotaur. From this it became a symbol of any victory and was taken over by Christianity as a symbol of hope. One tale tells that Mary gave birth to Jesus under a Palm Tree, and so a woman who has just given birth should eat three Dates.

The Babylonians must have known that the male and female Date Trees are separate, since an ancient bas relief shows an angel fertilizing a female tree with blossoms from a male. In many parts of the East it is the custom to assure fertilization by tying bunches of the male flowers near inflorescences on female trees. Both Theophrastus and Pliny had some inkling of the true state of affairs. According to the latter, "The more diligent inquirers into the operations of nature state that all trees belong to either the one sex or the other [wrong of course] . . . which manifests itself in no tree more than in the Palm". Yet, Mattioli agrees with Theophrastus that though there are indeed male and female Palms, both sometimes bear fruit!

Perhaps it was because of the obvious sexuality of the Palm that the Hindus are said to have believed it was just one step removed from the animal kingdom and endowed with intelligence. Yet, in the West it was not until the eighteenth century that plant sexuality was generally recognized, and as late as the middle of that century a professor of botany at Cambridge declared, "there is great reason to contend not only that all plants are not produced in a manner analogous to animal generation but that none are", thus giving another illustration of the fact that Cambridge, as well as Oxford, was a home of lost causes.

DATE PALM

Palmaceae : Phoenix

Mushroom

ALL THE FUNGI (*plants which can draw nourishment only from organic matter*) *were mysterious to the early botanists, and Dioscorides lumps all the thousands of species together, proposing only a very summary division: "Either they are edible or they are poisonous." This can hardly be questioned, but it is very nearly the only true statement he makes in the course of a short discussion, in which his explanation of why some are poisonous is especially picturesque: "Either they grow among rusty nails or rotten rags, or the holes of serpents, or amongst trees bearing harmful fruits."*

Mattioli dutifully repeats this bizarre theory but makes a much greater effort to suggest the existence of a bewildering number of species and to comment upon their use as food. His fellow Italians are, he says, determined to eat them, though "I am greatly astonished at the gourmandise and the disordered appetite of those who are so greedy for these Mushrooms which lead very often to death". Nevertheless, he undertakes to give some general rules for distinguishing the edible from the poisonous, much as some modern writers still do despite the usual opinion of the best authorities that there is no safety except in the ability to recognize positively the edible species. One sort of which the Tuscans are very fond is, he says, especially dangerous because it is so easily confused with another sort which is poisonous, though the two can be distinguished by their odor. According to Pliny they differ also in the way in which the flesh is discolored when it is cut. According to Avicenna one should avoid all that are black, green, or very dark red.

On his own responsibility Mattioli states that Mushrooms growing on trees are not dangerous "provided that the trees themselves are not poisonous". This, he explains, is because they come from the bark, where there can't be any rusty iron, or rotten rags, much less any snakes either dead or alive. And whatever one may think of the explanation, it is, I believe, usually true that fungi growing out of trees are non-poisonous, though not always edible.

Gerard repeats the warning which has been given so frequently (and so frequently in vain) ever since. "As we see and know many have eaten and do eat mushrooms rather for wantonness [Modern: 'for kicks'] than for need. There are two kinds thereof deadly; which being dressed by an unskilful cook may procure untimely death."

MUSHROOM

Various families: Agaricus

Juniper

ANY EXPERIMENT *in free association would probably demonstrate that some botanists and foresters would respond to the word "Juniper" with a reference to that well-known genus of gymnosperms often, but incorrectly, called Cedars. Nevertheless, many of even them, as well as most of the general public, would reply "Gin"—which word, by the way, is a corruption of "Geneva", which is, in turn, a misinterpretation of* Juniperus, *the classical Latin name for the tree.*

To the renaissance Herbalists, Juniper was, however, a medicinal plant, not an alcoholic liquor, for the good reason that (if one may trust the historians on the subject) Juniper berries were first used in the early seventeenth century by a son of Henry II of France to flavor a wine later distilled to make Gin. So many virtues were attributed to Juniper that Mattioli is moved to protest:

"Copies of Dioscorides in Greek are found in which the chapter on Geneva is entirely corrupted and confused with I know not what additions, not at all in the style of Dioscorides nor in that of his manner of teaching. I have never read, either in Galen or Aeginete or Serapion (who nevertheless have translated Dioscorides word by word) that the nutlets of the Geneva are fatal if taken in drink, that the seeds, if eaten are effective against snake bites, and that the leaves and their juice are applied to counteract the bite of vipers. Let me add that experiments indicate the contrary."

Despite this skepticism, some of the Herbalists continued to recommend Juniper as almost a complete pharmacy in itself. Here is Culpeper:

"This admirable Solar shrub can scarcely be equalled for its virtues. Its berries are hot in the third degree and dry in the first, being an excellent counter-poison and a great resister of pestilence . . . It is so powerful a remedy for the dropsy that by drinking only the lye made of the ashes of this herb it cures the disease." Moreover, he says, Juniper is good for the bite of venomous beasts; strengthens the stomach; expells wind; cures coughs, consumption, ruptures, cramps, and convulsions. It "strengthens the brain, helps memory and the optic nerves, speeds delivery of women, agues, gout and sciatica, hemorrhoids, worms, and falling sickness".

Is it any wonder that Martinis are popular today?

JUNIPER

Pinaceae : Juniperus

Viper

THOUGH THE HERBALISTS *deal primarily with plants, they also describe a certain number of mineral and animal substances supposed to be useful in the treatment of disease. Mattioli was an exact contemporary of Konrad Gesner, the first great European zoologist after Aristotle, and he often adds bits of natural history not to be found in Dioscorides.*

Thus, in the case of the Viper, he not only passes on recommendations from Dioscorides, Galen, and Marcellus the Empiricist, but doubts the statement that young vipers kill their mothers by gnawing their way out of the mother's belly. He also repeats Aristotle's remark that they shed their skin in spring and autumn, commencing with their eyes, so that they seem blind. (Actually it is before they shed that the opacity of the skin makes them seem blind.)

He says too that the flesh of the Viper, if boiled and eaten, is good for the eyes and is easier on the stomach if Spikenard is mixed with it. Boiled Viper also relieves toothache.

VIPER

Rye

THE ROMANS *knew a number of different grains but regarded most of them as very inferior to Wheat. They called one of them* Secale *and that is the modern scientific name for Rye, although it is not quite certain that this is what the ancients meant by* Secale. *Here is Pliny on the subject:*

"The people of Turin at the foot of the Alps give to Secale the name 'Asia'. It is a very poor food and serves only to avert starvation. Its stalk carries a large head but the straw is thin. It is dark in color and unusually heavy. Wheat is mixed with it to mitigate its bitter taste but even then it is disagreeable to the stomach. It will grow in any soil and yields a hundredfold. It is also employed as a green manure to enrich land."

What we call Rye is probably derived from a wild species found in the Mediterranean region. There is no evidence that it was cultivated in very ancient times and the names which it goes under suggest that it was first extensively grown in northern regions.

Gerard uses the name Rye and speaks of it unfavorably, though he was evidently much more familiar with it than Pliny was: "Rye groweth very plentifully in the moist places in Germany and Poland, as appeareth by the great quantity brought into England in time of dearth and scarcity of Corn, as happened in the year 1596 and at other times when there was a general want of Corn by reason of the abundance of rain that fell the year before; whereby great penury ensued as well of cattle and all other victuals as of all manner of grain. It groweth also very well in moist places of England, especially toward the north, . . . It is of a more clammy and obstructing nature than Wheat and harder to digest, yet to rustic bodies that can well digest it, it yields good nourishment." *Culpeper cites Mattioli as authority for the belief that* "the ashes of Rye straw, put into water and suffereth therein a day and a night will heal the chaps of the hands or feet".

Aside from this, Rye does not appear to have had much reputation as a medicinal plant, and this is one of the cases where what seemed unimportant to the Herbalist has become very important in modern medicine. Rye is the chief source of ergot, which is derived from a fungus attacking various grains but especially this one. It is an important crop in both Russia and the United States, though here its importance is chiefly as a forage and in the manufacture of Rye whiskey.

R Y E

Gramineae : Secale

Cork Oak

NOWADAYS, *the Cork Oak* (Quercus suber) *is grown commercially only in Spain, Portugal, and North Africa, where an area approximately that of New Jersey accounts for almost the entire world supply. The Greeks and Romans were well acquainted with its usefulness and Pliny describes it thus: "It is not a large tree . . . its thick bark grows again after being removed."*

It is, of course, upon this last curious fact that the usefulness of the Cork Oak depends. Other trees will die if the bark is removed because the movement of the sap is then disrupted. But in the case of the Cork Oak there are two layers of bark—an inner layer which functions like the bark of most trees, an outer which is merely a protective covering and can be removed without interfering with the normal life processes. Because of this fortunate arrangement it is possible to harvest the bark every eight to fifteen years, and a cork plantation furnishes an economically feasible crop.

It is no great wonder that Pliny permits himself a bit of teleological fantasy—which will outrage those modern biologists who vehemently deny any sort of purpose in Nature and, especially, that anything is intended for man's use: "When this tree is debarked it does not die as other trees do because Nature, like a farsighted mother, dressed it in a double bark, knowing well that it would be frequently debarked."

Though we still sometimes say "a cork" when we mean any kind of bottle stopper, cheaper metal or plastic substitutes have largely replaced those made of cork. Similarly, fiberglass tends to replace cork as a heat insulator.

CORK OAK

Fagaceae : Quercus

Horsetail

SOME TWO *or three hundred million years ago when the earth's "dry ground" was mostly a hot, humid swamp, many queer plants and many queer animals flourished, even though the first mammals and first flowers were still many millions of years away. One of the most conspicuous plants (some species reached a height of sixty feet) was a stiff, seemingly leafless, rush-like oddity sometimes bearing at its summit a cone which produced spores much like those of the ferns. Perhaps it should have become extinct millions of years ago, but it didn't, and only the very unobservant can have failed to see its modern descendants sometimes along a roadside or a railroad right-of-way. Except in size, they have changed almost not at all.*

Mattioli seems to have confused the Horsetails with another group of primitive plants, the Ephedra, *but one of his illustrations is accurate enough to be immediately recognizable. The root is perennial and, in spring, the cone-topped fruiting stems push their way up with almost irresistible force, often lifting stones or breaking the edges of tarred roads. Presently, they will drop spores which produce a flat green thallus bearing sex organs like those of the fern thallus, and out of this will grow the asexual generation of the Horsetail. Meanwhile, the sterile vegetative stem will have appeared as in the plate.*

The Herbalists who, of course, knew nothing of evolution and had very confused ideas about the possible sexuality of plants, suspected nothing of all this. To have called a plant "primitive" would have meant nothing, because even as late as Linnaeus it was still assumed that all living things had been created during the same wonderful week, and that the Garden of Eden was (as Linnaeus himself called it) the most complete botanical garden that had ever existed. All that the Herbalists could do was to describe the Equisetum *without understanding the meaning of its unusual form. Dioscorides calls our attention to its astringent properties, and remarks that it is sometimes used as a scouring reed for cooking pots and, more especially, by wood turners to polish their products. In Tuscany, during Lent, the peasants, he says, fry the tender shoots in oil or butter and eat them instead of fish.*

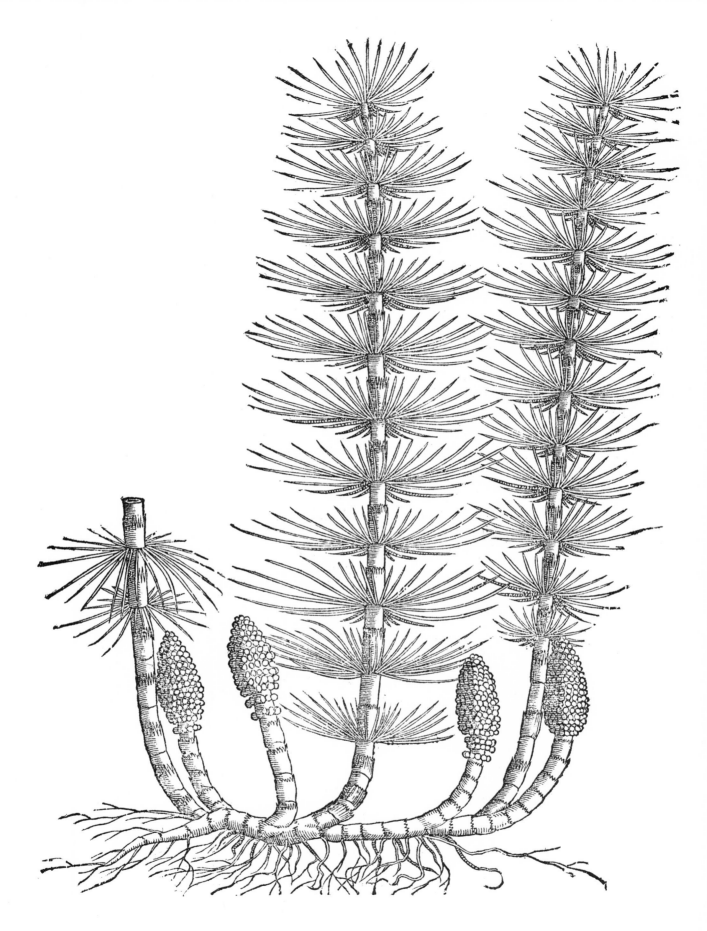

HORSETAIL

Equisetaceae: Equisetum

Navelwort

THERE ARE *two quite different plants sometimes called Navelwort in English: relatives of the Forget-me-not in the genus* Omphalodes *and members of the Sedum-Houseleek family in the genus* Cotyledon. *The drawing in the oldest manuscript of Dioscorides is highly schematic but it is evident that he is describing the* Cotyledons, *of which he gives two species; one being* C. umbilicus, *with round leaves to which the stem is attached in the middle, the other resembling a Hen-and-chickens* (Sempervivum). *Both grow in rocky places or in the chinks of walls, the first sometimes being cultivated in rock gardens.*

Mattioli, following Dioscorides, writes: "Its root is round like an olive. The juice mixed with wine and used to anoint the genital regions will depilitate the areas covered with hair. Used as a plaster it is good against inflamations, St. Anthony's Fire [erysipelas], and scrofula. Leaves and root if eaten break gall stones and cause urination. Mixed with honey they are also given to those suffering from dropsy. The herbaceous parts are employed in the works of love."

Gerard treats the Navelworts at some length and gives a variety of colloquial names: Navelwort, Wall Pennywort, Venus' Garden, Lady's Navel, Hipwort, and Kidneywort. He warns against ignorant apothecaries who confuse it with the poisonous Water Pennywort and thus endanger their patients.

The reason for the alternate name Pennywort is obvious, since the odd round leaves of C. umbilicus *are strikingly like coins. The appropriateness of Umbilicus Veneris is less obvious, though the round leaves do have a kind of dimple in the center. Perhaps this interpretation merely reflects the fascination which children and primitive people find in the navel. Buddha, of course, chose it as the subject of his longest meditation. In many mythologies it symbolizes the center of the earth. The Turks say that when the Devil saw the first man he spat at his stomach, and that the navel is the spot from which God quickly snatched away the pollution. Sir Thomas Browne discusses at some length the Vulgar Error of the painters who regularly give navels to Adam and Eve, despite the fact that, never having had umbilical cords, they could not have had navels.*

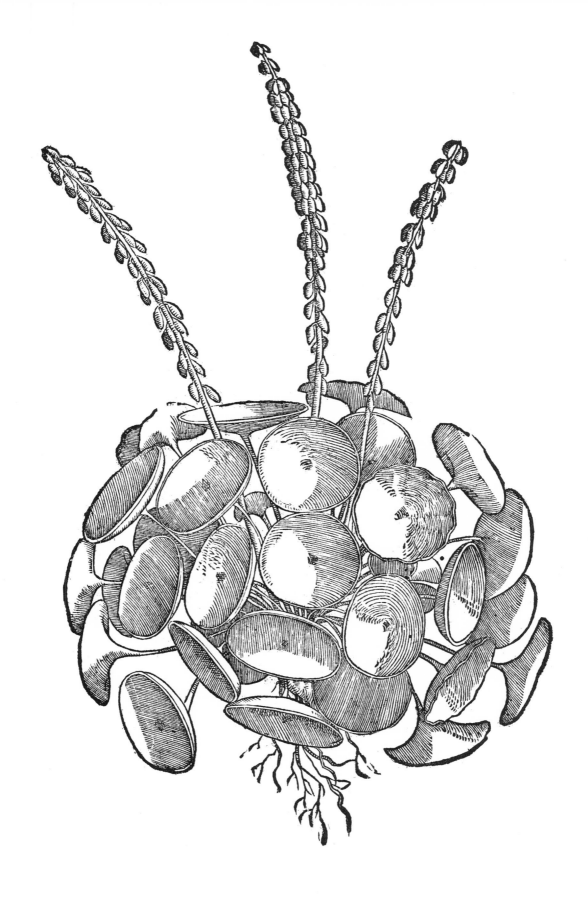

NAVELWORT

Crassulaceae : Cotyledon

Flax

LINNEAUS *gave the name* Linum usitatissimum *("most familiar")
to this species of the Flax genus, and none could have been more appropriate. Remnants found in the Swiss lake villages prove that man has
been familiar with it since the stone age, and though it was no doubt a
food plant first, the making of cloth from the fibers must have been one
of the earliest of domestic arts. Linen is found in the Egyptian tombs and
is mentioned in the* Odyssey *as well as in the Old Testament.*

*The learned monk Bartholomew of England describes how linen is
made. First the Flax plant is soaked, then dried, then "knocked, beaten
and brayed and carded, radded and gnodded, ribbed and heckled and at
last spun". It must have been manufactured in this manner, long, long
before Bartholomew's time, and the modern method is much the same.
The soft parts of the plant must be rotted away, the fibers separated,
combed, and finally spun.*

*Pliny, whose rhetorical outbursts and attempts at fine writing can be
exceptionally silly, begins a purple passage with the exclamation "What
department is to be found of active life in which flax is not employed?"
Then, referring to the linen sails of the Roman ships: "What audacity
in man! What criminal perverseness! Thus to sow a thing in the ground
for the purpose of catching the winds and tempests; it being not enough
for man to be borne along on the waves."*

*The Herbalists were, of course, principally concerned with the real and
supposed medicinal virtues of the Flax plant. According to Dioscorides
it has the power of "mollifying all inflamation inwardly and outwardly,
being sod [boiled] with honey and oil and a little water or being taken
inwardly sod with honey". As a cataplasm with honey and figs it is good
for sunburn and mixed with honey and pepper "doeth also provoke
venery".*

*Today, old-fashioned doctors order linseed when a hot poultice is indi-
cated and would not find much to disagree with in Culpeper's statement: "[The seed] being boiled in water and applied as a poultice or
plaster assuageth all pains, softeneth cold, tumors or swellings, the im-
postumes of the neck and other parts of the body . . . pounded with
figs, it is good to ripen and bring to a head boils and other swellings."*

FLAX

Linaceae : Linum

Lily

"THE LILY", *wrote the thirteenth-century encyclopedist Bartholomew of England, "is next the Rose in worthiness and nobleness . . . Nothing is more gracious in fairness of color, in sweetness of smell and in effect of working and virtue."*

In this he was echoing Pliny as well as the common opinion from ancient times down to his own and beyond. According to Semitic traditions, a Lily sprang up where Eve dropped a tear on leaving Eden. A Korean Androcles removed an arrow from the foreleg of a tiger; they became friends; and when the tiger died he begged the hermit to use his magic to keep him nearby. His body became the Tiger Lily and when the hermit was drowned the Lily spread over the land looking for him. The white Madonna Lily is sacred to the Virgin Mary and is said to have been yellow until she stooped to pick it. On the other hand, what the English Bible translates as "the Lilies of the field" were, so modern botanists agree, certainly not Lilies at all. Gerard argues that they were probably Tulips, but the prevalent guess favors some kind of Anemone.

The Lily described by Dioscorides is accompanied in the oldest manuscript by a drawing so debased as to be almost unrecognizable, but, like that reproduced here, is probably the Madonna Lily (Lilium candidum), *native to southern Europe and Asia. Dioscorides says about the medicinal virtues of the Lily that it is good against both new and old wounds; with Hysccyamus and Wheat flower it soothes inflamation of the testicles and is, like so many other things, an antidote against snake bite.*

Mattioli is concerned more with the Lily as an ornamental, citing Pliny's celebration of its excellence and its effectiveness when planted with Roses, which last are beginning to fade when the Lily comes into bloom. He adds that he would like to describe the method used by the ancients to turn the white Lily red, but then changes the subject, presumably implying that this interesting art has been lost. Then he mentions various other plants which he thinks resemble Lilies, including the Crinums, *which do belong to the same family, and the* Convolvulus, *which is very remote from it.*

It is said that in England, and in many parts of the United States, a folk belief holds that to smell Lilies (especially Tiger Lilies) will produce freckles—certainly an interesting example of sympathetic magic.

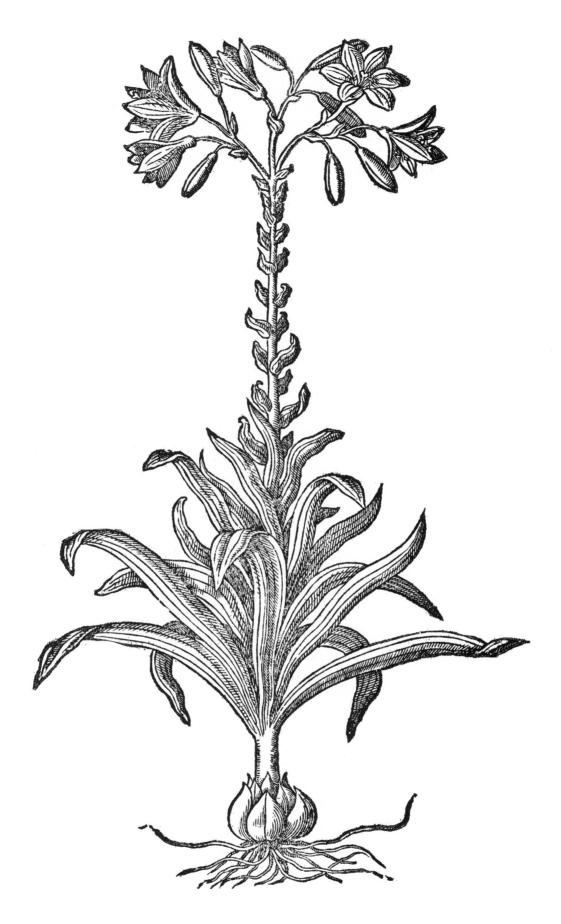

LILY

Liliaceae : Lilium

Woodfern

THE EARLIEST HERBALISTS *called this type of Fern* Polypodium, *and that is still the scientific as well as the semi-popular name for any of the many species of Woodfern. The name means "many-footed" and refers to the branched "root" characteristic of the species. Though members of the immense genus are scattered all over the world and differ enormously among themselves, ours grow on rocks, in the woods, or especially on tree trunks. Mattioli's description very well fits those familiar to walkers in our woods:*

"The Polypody grows on mossy rocks and on the trunks of old trees, especially on Oaks . . . Its root is thick and bears certain nodules the size of a little finger and similar to those one sees on an octopus[!]." He adds that the Polypody is laxative, but to be effective must be cooked with chicken, fish, Mallow, or Beets. It seems to have been the usual opinion that Polypodys growing on Oak were the best.

Naturally, the Herbalists were intrigued and puzzled by the rows of dots on the backs of some fronds and by the dust which came from them. It is not surprising that this dust was not recognized as reproductive spores since they do not produce ferns directly, and the small flat thallus they do produce (and from which the Fern ultimately grows) is both inconspicuous and not likely to be associated with the Fern.

Coles, one of the Herbalists most interested in "signatures" writes: "The rough spots that are on the underside of the leaves of Polypody, as also the knags or excrescences on each side of the roots, is a sign that it is good for the lungs and the exulcerations thereof."

Possibly just because the spores and spore cases seemed to have no function they were—and in places still are—assigned various magical properties and associated with various superstitions. Since these "seeds" are nearly invisible, they will render invisible those who eat them or, sometimes, even those who carry them. Because Ferns bear no flowers, it was believed that they bloomed only on Midsummer's Eve and that the large golden flower produced at that time had extraordinary characteristics, varying from country to country. One tale was that anyone who climbs a mountain with the golden flower in his hand will find there a gold hoard or have the location of such a hoard revealed to him in a vision.

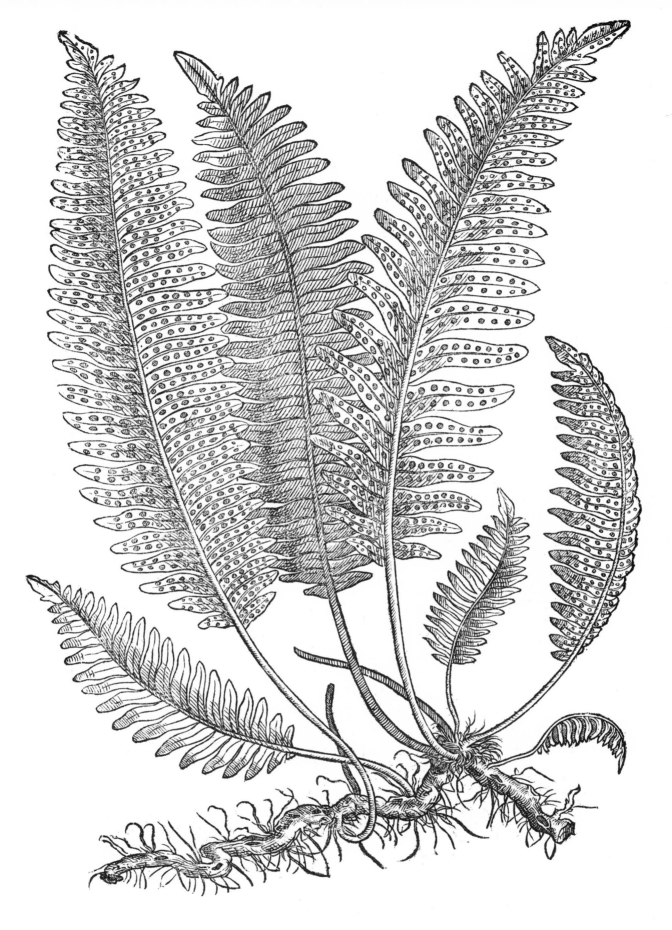

WOODFERN

Polypodiaceae: Polypodium

Houseleek

A GREAT VARIETY *of names both learned and popular have been given to different groups of this enormous family composed of succulent herbs and a few sub-shrubs. It includes something like nine hundred species, many of which we call Houseleeks or, in the case of those which put out offshoots from a basal rosette, Hen-and-chickens. House-leeks are also called Sempervivums by the Herbalists because they are mostly evergreen, and this name has been retained for one of the modern genera.*

One is tempted to say that their most usual habitat is city apartments, where they are commonly found in dish gardens; but in the olden days they were often planted between the tiles of a roof, and from this comes the technical name Sempervivum tectorum *for what is probably the most familiar of the various Hens-and-chickens.*

Mattioli pictures several sorts, at least two of which appear to belong to the modern genus Sedum *and three which he calls* Sempervivum majus. *One of these may be the modern* Sempervivum arborem *(a native of the Mediterranean region) while the others are different enough in appearance to be, perhaps, other species. All the members of the family are bland and inoffensive, hence not credited with many sensational medicinal virtues. They have, however, played a role in magic.*

Charlemagne is said to have made it a law that Houseleeks should be planted on the roof of every house. This requirement was probably not so much to assure every householder a handy supply of medicine as to take advantage of the Houseleek's magical potency. It was a Celtic superstition that it brought good luck and, especially, that it protected a building from lightning—a superstition which must have been still alive eight hundred years after Charlemagne's day, since Culpeper (though not given to doubting the miraculous) says: "Jove claims dominion over this herb from which it is fabulously reported that it preserves whatever it grows upon from fire and lightning."

Perhaps Charlemagne had heard also of the magico-medical virtue described in the Hortus Sanitatis, *where it is said that if the juice of the Houseleek be mixed with the milk of a woman who is nursing a boy ten or twelve weeks old, and if just two or three drops of the mixture be dropped into the ear of a deaf person, his hearing will be restored "without fail".*

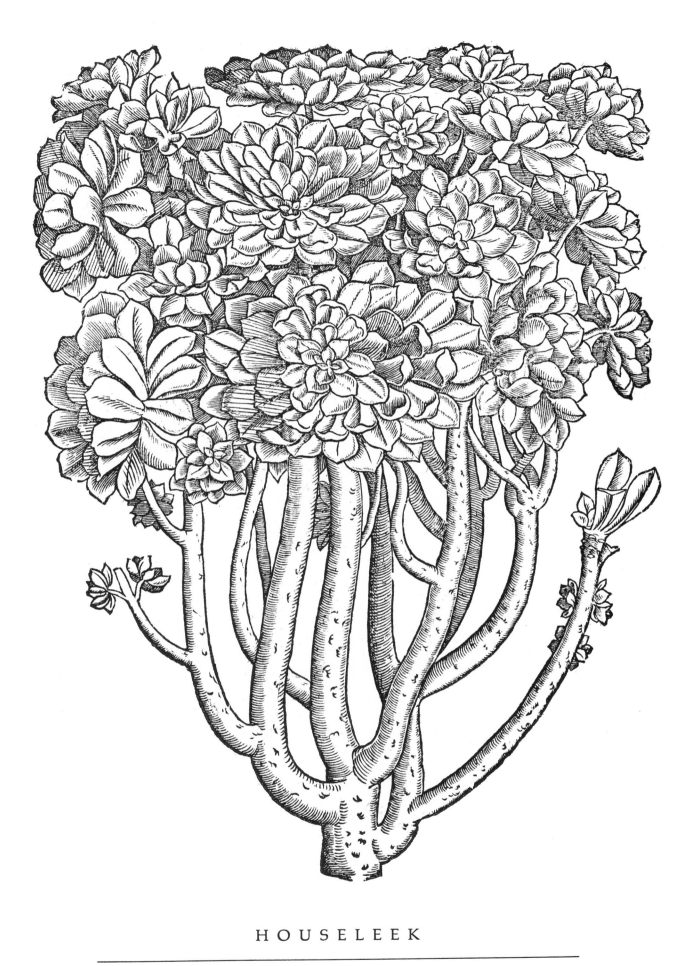

HOUSELEEK

Crassulaceae : Sempervivum

Nasturtium

THE MOST CASUAL GARDENER *will be astonished to see the name of a familiar garden flower given to this humble weed. Actually, however, what we call a Nasturtium was unknown to the ancients, who gave the name to various of the Cresses for the very good reason that it means "nose twister", in reference to the pungency common to members of the Mustard family.*

Pliny lists forty-two medicinal uses and records this improbable belief: "Sextius adds that the smell of burnt Nasturtium drives away serpents, neutralizes the venom of scorpions . . . Mixed with oil and applied to the ears with fig in it, is a remedy for hardness of hearing."

Dioscorides lumps a number of the Cresses together and says that "the seed of any sort . . . is warming, sharp, bad for the stomach, troubling the belly, and expelling worms, lessening the spleen, killing the embryo, moving the menstrua, exciting to copulation". Charlemagne included it among the herbs which he ordered his subjects to cultivate.

Mattioli distinguishes several kinds, but what he calls Sisymbrium aquaticum *seems to be our Water Cress, of which the official generic name has been several times changed by modern botanists—from* Sisymbrium, *to* Nasturtium, *to* Radicula. *We use it principally as a "garnish", to be consumed by some without fear of either a positive (according to Dioscorides) or a negative (according to Pliny) aphrodisiacal effect.*

The introduction of our garden Nasturtium is sometimes credited to the sixteenth-century Spaniard whose book was translated into English under the exuberant title Joyous News Out of the New Found World *—in which tobacco was given first place as something approaching a cure-all. Gardeners enthusiastically adopted the easily grown flower and called it "the Indian Nose Twister", though botanists now put it in a different family and call the common species* Tropaeolum majus.

Gerard speaks enthusiastically of its beauty. Parkinson calls it Nasturtium Indicum *or* Lark's Heels, *because it has "spurs or heeles". "It is of so great beauty and sweetness . . . that my gardens of delight [i.e. as opposed to a medical garden] cannot be unfurnished of it."*

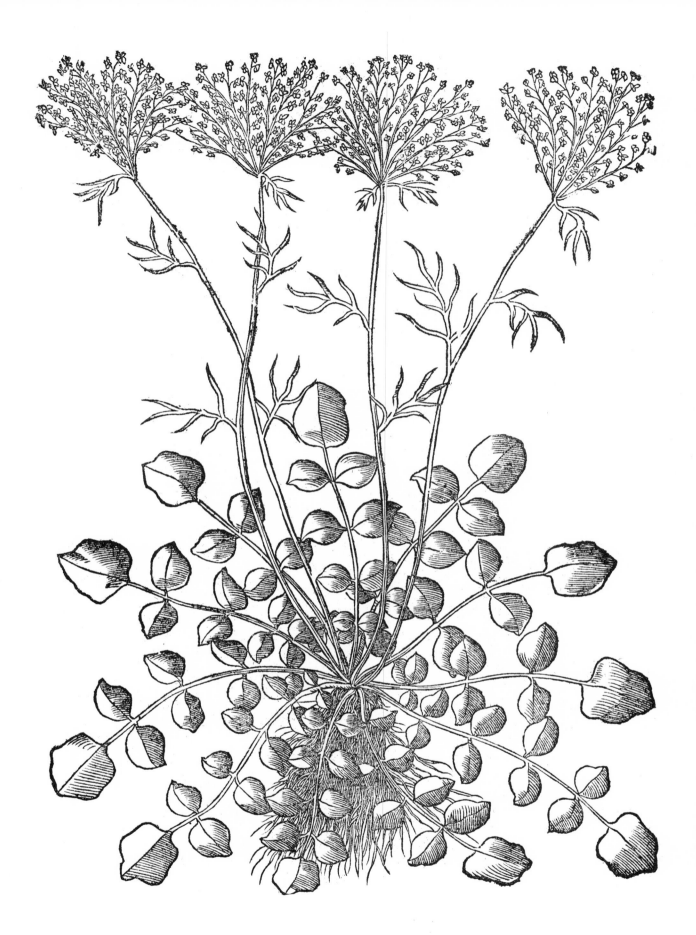

NASTURTIUM

Cruciferae : Radicula

Plane Tree

90

"THE TREES AND FORESTS", *writes Pliny, "were supposed to be the supreme gift bestowed by Nature on man . . . They first provided him with his food; their foliage carpeted his cave; and their bark served him for raiment . . . We use a tree to furrow the seas and bring the lands nearer together; we use a tree for building houses; even the images of the gods were made from trees . . . But who is there who will not with good reason be surprised to learn that a tree has been introduced among us for nothing but its shade? I mean the Plane which was first brought across the Ionian Sea . . . and was afterwards imported thence into Sicily, being one of the first exotic trees that were introduced into Italy."*

It is one of Pliny's peculiarities that he swallows without blinking the most fantastic tales, and then laboriously works up far-fetched wonderment over something no more extraordinary than the planting of a tree for its shade. Still, the Plane (similar to our Sycamore) was indeed a great favorite in the ancient world because of the unusually large size it attains when given enough water. Homer and Virgil both refer to it in terms of admiration and there are various other stories told about the pains taken to cultivate and honor it. Agamemnon planted a Plane at Delphi. It was to a Plane that the Satyr Marsayas was tied when Apollo flayed him alive for daring to challenge the god to a musical contest. At Candia, in Crete, they showed the Plane tree under which Jupiter violated Europa. According to the Roman sophist Aelian, Xerxes, on his expedition against Greece, threw caution to the winds and wasted a whole day in Lydia because he could not resist the shade of a magnificent Plane. Pliny remarks also that his compatriots had made even trees into winebibbers by watering the Planes with wine in the belief that it would encourage their growth. A certain Licinius Mutianus, Governor of Lycia, was so taken with a giant Plane tree, hollow at its base like a great cavern, that he sometimes feasted there with as many as eighteen companions.

The Plane tree is seen often in large cities, this being one of the few kinds able to thrive in such inhospitable conditions.

PLANE TREE

Platanaceae : Platanus

Indian Fig

OF THE NATURAL WONDERS *brought to Europe from the New World, none amazed and confused the botanists more than the Prickly Pear of the American deserts. Introduced into other lands, it now flourishes (sometimes all too exuberantly) in regions as remote from one another as Africa and Australia, but no member of the family is native outside the Western Hemisphere.*

Theophrastus mentions an odd prickly plant which he says grew near an African village called Opuns, and sixteenth-century Herbalists assumed that this was the same as the strange Indian Fig then recently brought from the New World. It seems pretty certain, however, that Theophrastus is describing one of the African Euphorbias, *which have come to resemble the Cacti because they have developed many of the same adaptations to aridity. As a result of the ensuing confusion, one of the largest genera of the Cactus family now bears the inappropriate scientific name* Opuntia, *derived from that of the African town.*

Since the fruit of the Prickly Pear somewhat resembles that of the Fig Tree, the Herbalists classified it with the Figs, though Mattioli himself seems somewhat dubious. "It is certainly just to put it among the miracles of nature in view of an almost incredible fact: The leaves are often thicker than the thumb and are all provided with small spines which are white, thin, long, and pointed."

A piece of the "leaf", he goes on, will put forth others if planted. Those who eat the red fruit for the first time are frightened by the fact that their urine becomes red.

In early seventeenth-century England, horticulturists like Gerard and Parkinson were eager to propagate such a curiosity as the Cactus. The former grew also Tomatoes from America and Nasturtiums from the Indies, as well as Tobacco and the Prickly Pear. Of the latter he says: "In Italy it sometimes beareth fruit, but more often in Spain and never yet in England, although I have bestowed great pains and cost in keeping it from injury by our cold climate." Parkinson also reports that the fruit always remains green in England.

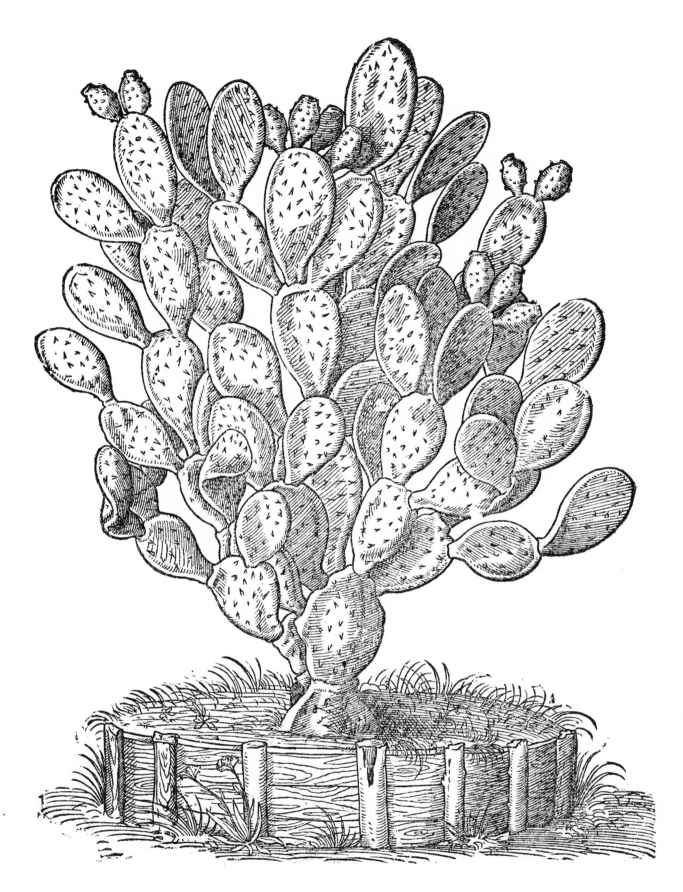

INDIAN FIG

Cactaceae: Opuntia

Thyme

THYME *is a European herb (or rather shrub) of the Mint family which has never become naturalized in the United States, though the two species known to the Herbalists as the Common and the Creeping are both familiar to gardeners. It is also unusual among the old-fashioned herbs in that it plays a new role of importance in modern medicine.*

Mattioli describes the distillation of a golden Oil of Thyme. Today, a stearoptene called Thymol is obtained by the evaporation of this oil. It is an antiseptic resembling carbolic acid and has various minor uses, including those of a mouth wash and a gargle. But its most important use is in the treatment of Hookworm, against which it is said to be almost a specific.

The ancient and medieval Herbalists found other medicinal uses for Thyme. Pliny, for instance, lists twenty-eight disorders for which it is a remedy, his most remarkable prescription being for epileptics, who are advised not only to sniff but also to sleep upon it. Mattioli, citing the authority of Galen, recommends it for a wide variety of ills. It induces both urination and the menstrual flow; also provokes abortion. It loosens discharges of the chest or lungs and purges choler or black humour, being therefore useful to the melancholic.

From Greek times down to the present, Thyme has been used as a flavoring for food also, but one gets the feeling that it has always been even more popular for its beauty and its odor. It was usually a component of the garlands of which the Greeks were so fond. These were sold in special markets, one of which is described by Athenaeus as a place where the freshly bathed shoppers "babble before the wreath market or gabble at the perfume booths". And in one of the surviving fragments from the Greek dramatist, Euboulos, a girl thus recommends wreaths of Thyme: "Who could forbear to kiss/ A girl who's wearing this?" Indeed, poets from ancient times to the present seem to have had an especial fondness for Thyme; as witness Ovid's "Purple hills of flowering Hymettus", Shakespeare's "I know a bank where the wild Thyme blows", and Milton's "Desert caves with wild Thyme and gadding vine o'ergrown".

Halfway between the utilitarian and the poetic is Thyme's fame as the source of the finest Honey, especially that from Mount Hymettus in Attica.

THYME

Labiatae: Thymus

Leek

IN LATIN, *the Leek was called* Porrum, *hence the specific part of its modern name,* Allium porrum. *As is so often the case, the gossipy and credulous Pliny supplies the oddest anecdotes concerning this humble vegetable.*

"It has recently acquired considerable celebrity from the use made of it by the Emperor Nero. That Prince, to improve his voice, used to eat Leeks and oil every month upon stated days, abstaining from every other kind of food and not even touching so much as a morsel of bread."

Since both Aristotle and Dioscorides recommend Leeks to improve the voice, Nero was merely following their advice in preparation for one of his appearances as a singer. Pliny then goes on to tell another story obviously reflecting the somewhat sinister reputation of the whole Onion tribe:

"There is a story told that Mela [brother of Seneca and father of Lucan], a member of the Equestrian order, being accused of maladministration by order of the Emperor Tiberius, swallowed in his despair Leek juice to the amount of three silver denarii in weight and expired upon the spot without the slightest symptom of pain. It is said, however, that a larger dose than this is productive of no injurious effects whatsoever."

Dioscorides says that Leeks dull the sight, produce nightmares, and are bad for the stomach, but he also grants them a very miscellaneous assortment of medicinal virtues. The leaves boiled in sea water are good against hardness of the womb (whatever that may be). The juice mixed with Frankincense stops blood, especially that which comes from the nose, "provokes to venery" and, mixed with honey, is prescribed for all disorders of the thorax, including consumption. Like so many other plants, it also was credited with giving protection against the bite of venomous beasts. The number of herbs said to be effective against this misfortune suggests that there were not very many really venomous beasts about in Greece or Rome.

LEEK

Liliaceae : Allium

Bindweed

IN POPULAR SPEECH *we are likely to call all the twining* Convolvuluses *Morning Glories, but that name properly belongs to only one genus* (Ipomoea) *and is, besides, of recent American origin, being first recorded by the Oxford Dictionary as of 1836. Many of its members are twining and this is the significance of the Latin name* Convolvulus *and of the Greek* Helixine.

Of the plate which faces this page, Mattioli says that he is quite sure it is a Convolvulus *but not sure which one. Almost certainly it is one of those given in Dioscorides and identical with the modern* C. arvensis. *The latter was accidentally introduced into the United States and now flourishes extravagantly, both where its white flowers are a modest ornament to waste ground and where its twining stems are a serious pest in cultivated fields.*

An old name used in England (by Turner, for example) was Withwinde, and this is an indication that a curious fact had been noted, namely that all members of this family twine counterclockwise, the first syllable of the old popular name being the same as in "Withershins". All of the Honeysuckles, on the other hand, twine clockwise. Modern biology says that the necessity of turning one way or another is locked in the genes, but our ancestors, who were more poetical than scientific, were aware only of the fact that when a Bindweed and a Honeysuckle happen to twine about one another they are joined in a very tight embrace. Ben Jonson makes a metaphor out of this and so does Shakespeare, who has Titania wind Bottom in her arms as tightly as "doth the Woodbine, the sweet Honeysuckle".

C. arvensis *is bland and has no medicinal value, but many members of the family, especially those which produce large tubers, contain potent alkaloids. Dioscorides knew at least one of these which was imported from Asia and called Skammonia* (C. scammonia), *a very violent purgative still sometimes used in medicine under the name Jalap. Gerard says of it that "there is not any plant growing upon the earth knowledge of which more concerneth the physician than this Scammony . . . and though the herb is suspected and half condemned of some men, yet there is not another herb to be found whereof so small a quantity will do so much good".*

BINDWEED

Convolvulaceae : Convolvulus

Mandrake

A WHOLE BOOK *could be written—in fact, a whole modern book* has *been written*—on the Mandrake, that most famous and most sensational of all the plants which figure in medicine and magic. A member of the Tomato-Nightshade family, it yields a powerful alkaloid very similar to Belladona and can produce delirium, but the only explanation which can be offered for the extraordinary elaboration and persistence of superstitions concerning it is the fact that the root is sometimes forked. This very vague suggestion of a human body stimulated the imagination (and also the ingenuity of charlatans) until some serious medieval books (the late fifteenth-century* Hortus Sanitatis, *for example) represent the plant as a perfectly detailed male or female human figure, with leaves and small round fruits springing from the head.*

Many of the superstitions concerning it occur in the folklore of widely separated peoples and were certainly very ancient when perpetuated by the classical writers. According to one theory, the Mandrake is generated when the body drippings from a gibbet sink into the ground. When pulled out of the ground, it drips blood and utters a shriek which will either prove fatal to the hearer, or, according to another version, drive him mad.

Theophrastus details, without necessarily giving full credence to, the precautions to be taken by those who collect the Mandrake—which was obviously a more "dreadful trade" than that of gathering Samphire as described in King Lear. One should draw a circle three times around the plant while reciting some sort of incantation; or, as some other authorities recommend, have it pulled up by a dog, who will then go mad in place of his master.

Among other magical powers of the Mandrake were those of an aphrodisiac and a promoter of conception so powerful that it was effective if merely placed under a bedspread. To this last "virtue" the English translation of Genesis pays tribute in the story of Leah and Jacob, though the plant referred to in Hebrew is a "love apple", which may or may not have been the Mandrake. According to one of the medieval Bestiaries, elephants are devoid of sexual desire unless they stimulate themselves with Mandrake. On the other hand, if a bear is so ill advised as to eat the fruits of this same plant, he will die unless he quickly eats ants as a restorative.

* *The Mystic Mandrake,* Charles John Thompson, London, 1931.

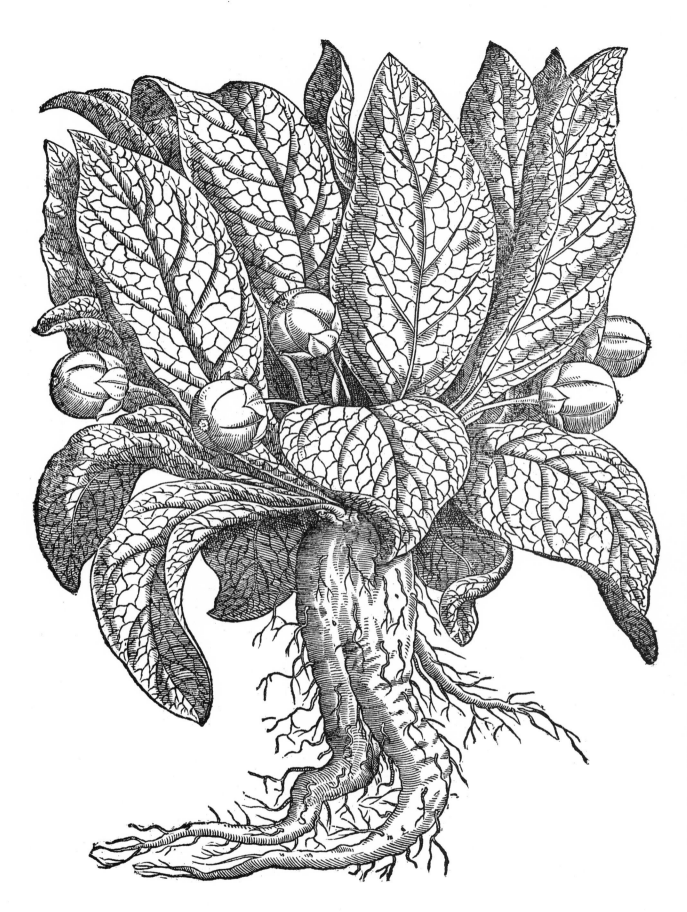

MANDRAKE

Solanaceae : Mandragora

Mandrake

TRUTH CRUSHED TO EARTH *may rise again, but somewhat less stubbornly than picturesque fictions which appeal to the human imagination more strongly than does sober fact. So far as the record goes, skepticism concerning the miraculous characteristics of the Mandrake is almost as old as the fables. Theophrastus cannot swallow the whole story; Dioscorides mentions none of its most sensational features; and the other Herbalists, one after another, ridicule it. As far back as the thirteenth century, Bartholomew retells some of the legends but concludes with the phrase, "It is so feined of churles". Turner (1541) rejects the common belief that a Mandrake root is shaped like a human being. Gerard (1597), after recording the superstitions, concludes: "All which dreams and old wives tales you should henceforth cast out of your books and memory." Yet, a century later, Sir Thomas Browne in his encyclopedia of Vulgar Errors is still combatting the legend by retelling Mattioli's account of what he learned of the methods of a "vagabond cheater" whom he was treating for "the French disease". To deceive unfruitful women, he carried about a sort of doll carved from the fresh root of Briony, into which he had planted Barley or Millet seeds where he wanted hair to grow. Then such swindlers "bury them in sand until the grains shoot from their roots; . . . they afterwards clip and trim these tender strings in the fashion of beards and other hairy tegument".*

Despite all the superstitions, the alkaloid present is, among other things, a powerful if dangerous anodyne and it was genuinely effective for certain, if not all, of the purposes for which it was given. Pliny refers to patients given the root to chew as an anesthetic, and Dioscorides recommends it both for those who cannot sleep and those who are "grievously pained". It is also said to "infatuate" (i.e. cause hallucinations), and this also is true.

Shakespeare and his contemporaries were well aware of the aura of wonder and mystery surrounding the Mandrake. Juliet fears that if she wakes in the tomb she will be terrified by shrieks "like Mandrakes torn out of the earth". Cleopatra exclaims, "Give me to drink mandragora . . ./ That I might sleep out this great gap of time/ My Anthony is away". Donne, daring the hearer to try impossibilities, exclaims, "Get with child a Mandrake root!"

MANDRAKE

Solanaceae : Mandragora

Gourd

THE GOURDS *belong in the same family (some in the same genus) with the Melons, the Squashes, and Cucumbers. Nearly all the family are tendril bearing and all produce separate male and female flowers. They are enormously variable under cultivation, hybridize freely, and thus run into innumerable varieties grouped in the approximately seven hundred botanically recognizable species.*

Ordinarily, we call "Gourd" those which are inedible but either ornamental or useful; "Melon" those which are sweet; and "Squash", "Cucumber", etc., those which are edible but not sweet. The ancients were familiar with various types, but it is often impossible to say which of the varieties they mention correspond to our recognized species and named varieties.

Pliny treats the Gourds at length, describing various kinds and also giving cultural directions. "The Gourd", he writes, "admits of being applied to more numerous uses than even the cucumber: the stem is used as an article of food when young, but at a later date it changes its nature and becomes entirely different; of late, Gourds have come to be used in baths for jugs and pitchers, but for this long time past they have been employed for keeping wine".

Presumably because Gourds do not come dependably true from seed he is misled into the belief that: "The seeds which lie nearest the neck of the Gourd produce fruit of remarkable length, and so do those which lie at the lower extremities, though not at all comparable with the others. Those, on the other hand, which lie in the middle produce Gourds of a round shape and those at the sides of the fruit are thick and short."

Despite all the confusion of classification, the type pictured opposite is recognizably one of those cultivated today—chiefly as an ornament or a curiosity.

The late, great horticultural authority, Liberty Hyde Bailey, calls attention to this fact in his The Garden of Gourds, *where he writes under the heading "Bottle and Dumbell": "Gourds constricted in the center . . . the lower end much enlarged and globular, the upper part above the isthmus not thick. This name represents a general shape rather than size or season . . ." The bottle form is shown in the upper fruits of the plate.*

GOURD

Cucurbitaceae : Cucurbita

Cattail

TYPHA *was the ancient Greek name for this familiar but odd looking as well as botanically odd plant. The early English Herbalists sometimes called it Reedmace, but more usually it was named what it is still called today: Cattail. Nowadays it is also often called Bulrush, and that immediately suggests the infant Moses. But this is misleading. He, so it is generally supposed, was concealed in a Papyrus thicket, not among the Cattails.*

"Typha", says Mattioli, "is so well known that there is no use giving a detailed description". That statement is in certain ways more amply justified than he knew, for a single species, Typha latifolia *(that to which both he and Dioscorides apparently refer) is of world wide distribution and is no more at home in Greece or in Italy than it is in the United States.*

To modern botanists it is, nevertheless, a bit of a puzzle. Despite its obvious superficial resemblance to the Reeds and the Rushes it is actually a flowering plant, and is now put in a separate family called the Typhaceae, *which consists of only the one genus,* Typha.

The tiny flowers which win it this distinction are of the utmost simplicity—the petals and sepals being represented by a few mere bristles. These tiny flowers are of separate sexes, placed one above the other on the same stem. Wind carries pollen to a neighboring stem and the red-brown cylinder which we find so decorative is composed of thousands of tiny seeds. The system of plant classification now generally accepted puts Typha *among the very first of the flowering plants and therefore, by implication at least, related to the very first such plants to develop.*

Galen does not mention Typha *among the medicinal herbs; Dioscorides gives it only a few lines; and Mattioli obviously considers its non-medicinal uses as at least as important as its medicinal. "There are few bodies of still water where this plant is not found. The down which it bears is called in Italian Mazza sorda, because if it falls on a person's ears it renders him deaf. Poor people use this down to stuff and make soft their bed pillows." He also describes, without seeming to vouch for, a common use of the down as part of an elaborate recipe for the treatment of hernias.*

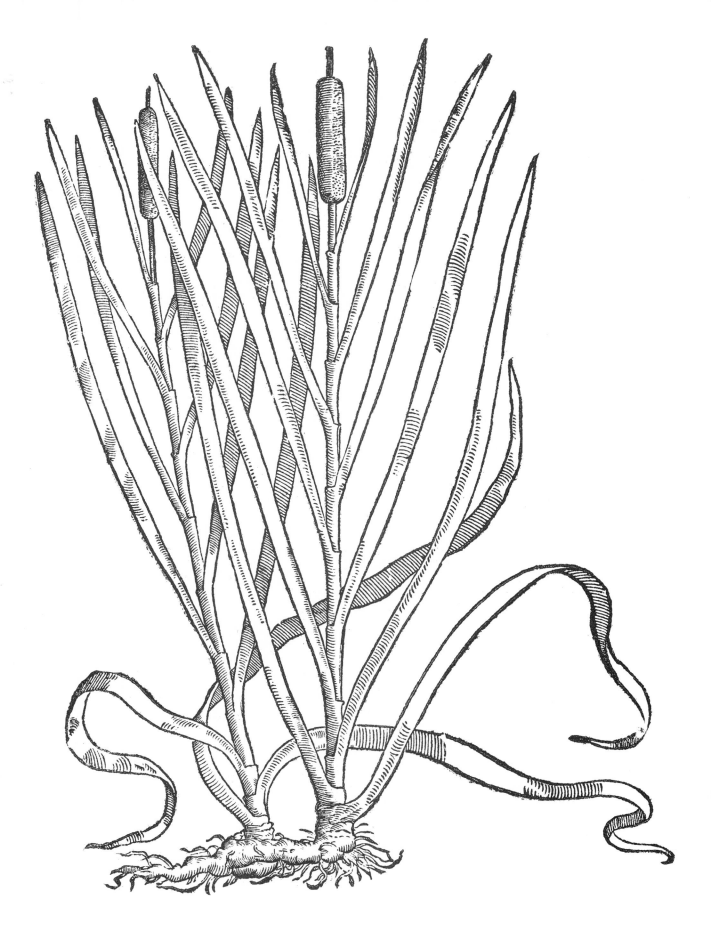

CATTAIL

Typhaceae : Typha

Clove

THE EARLY GREEKS, *says Coles, had no name for the Clove but the Latins called it* Clavus, *because of its resemblance to a small nail. This is correct enough if you understand by "the Latins" the late inhabitants of the dying Roman Empire. Neither Pliny nor Dioscorides had ever tasted what was to become one of the most popular of the spices. It is said to have been first brought into Europe sometime between the fourth and the sixth centuries* A.D., *and few, if any, other plants ever exercised upon the history of the Christian Era so strong an influence.*

After all, Columbus did not expect to find Tobacco, but it was the desire for spices which sent men in search of an ocean route to "the Indies". The Arabs held a monopoly on the trade in Cloves until the sea route around Africa was discovered in the sixteenth century. Then first the Portuguese, and after them the Dutch, attempted to maintain a monopoly by control of the sea lanes and by destroying the tree everywhere except in the Mollucas, which seem to have been the native home of the Clove.

To Coles, the Clove was almost equally important as a medicine and as a food spice: "[They] help the memory, eyesight and concoction and strengthen nature; they break wind, stir up venery or a bodily lust . . . They are good against the plague . . . they strengthen the retentive faculty and make the breath sweet and stay vomiting." They are also, he adds, good against the toothache and that, of course, is one of the uses to which Oil of Cloves is still put. Cloves are also much used, Coles continues, in broths and sauces. Nowadays, the household hints departments in newspapers and magazines sometimes describe the apple, orange or lemon stuck full of cloves, but this is not a very novel invention since in Love's Labor's Lost *we find:*

> *The omnipotent Mars, of lances the almighty,*
> *Gave Hector a gift, a gilt nutmeg, a lemon stuck with Cloves.*

Coles also recommends decorating a roast by sticking cloves over the surface.

This spice is unique in being the only one which is neither a seed like Nutmeg, a root like Ginger, nor a bark like Cinnamon, but an unopened bud which has been dried with its stem attached.

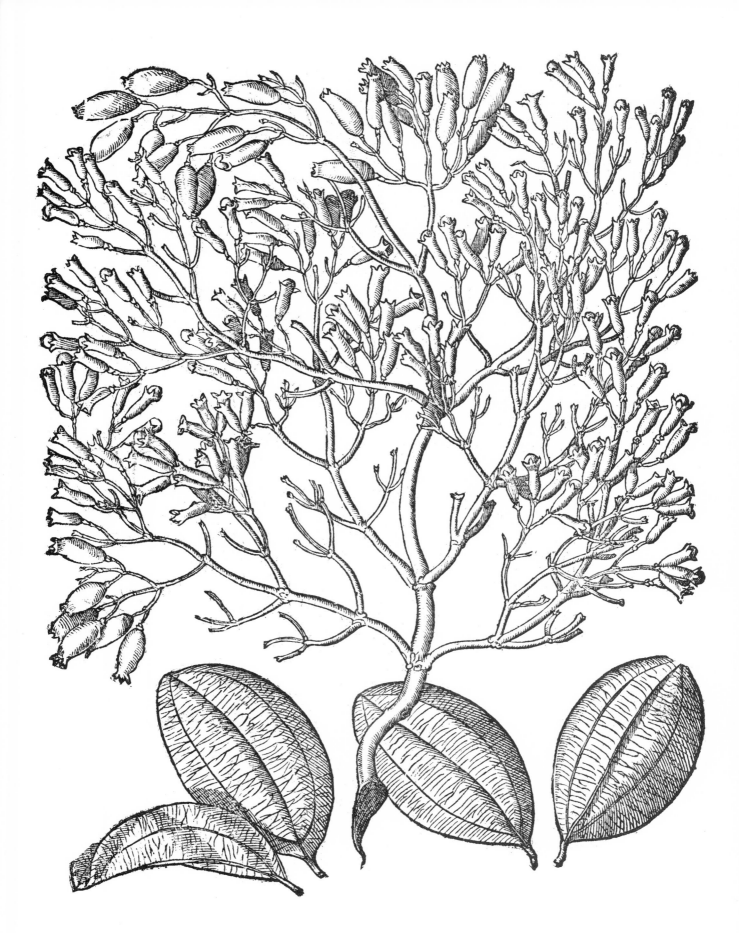

CLOVE

Myrtaceae : Eugenia

Cabbage

110

THE CABBAGES ARE, *like Wheat and Maize, among the greatest gifts of prehistoric man to his modern descendants. All three are cultigens and all three have been grown for thousands of years. Hence they are so changed from their original forms that it is impossible to be sure from what wild parents they are descended.*

Candolle, the first great student of the origins of cultivated plants, thought that our garden Cabbages were of mixed ancestry and that the mixture included several wild species still found along certain sea coasts. The informed guess of some later students is that only the Sea Cabbage (B. oleracea) *is involved. In any case, no wild species resembles the cultivated vegetable at all closely and, though it cannot be older than the Neolithic period when men first cultivated crops, it may have begun its evolution in the Middle East about that time—say eight or ten thousand years ago.*

All our cultivated kinds are now usually regarded as mere varieties of B. oleracea. *Different as they appear, the Kales, Cauliflowers, and Broccolis are also taken to be merely other varieties of the same species. Within the same genus are the Kohlrabies, the Turnips, and the Rutabagas. Pliny, Theophrastus, and before them Cato, described a number of kinds, all of which make it evident that the family to which* Brassica *belongs was, like certain other plant and animal families, genetically unstable, and therefore subject to frequent mutations of which the plant breeder could take advantage. Perhaps the* Cruciferae (Mustards) *have not contributed as much to human welfare as Wheat and Maize, but mankind could not well have spared them. In the eighteenth century it was another member of the family called Scurvy Grass* (Cochlearia) *which mitigated the horror of long sea voyages by acting as an effective antiscorbutic.*

Of the Cabbages as food and as medicine Mattioli writes: "Garden Cabbages only slightly cooked are good for the stomach, but if they are cooked too long, and especially if they are cooked with soda or cooked twice, they contract it . . . They are good for those afflicted with tremblings and those whose eyesight is troubled. Eaten at the end of a meal they remove all the effects of drinking too much wine . . . With salt they cause carbuncles to burst and keep in hair which is tending to fall."

CABBAGE

Cruciferae : Brassica

Orange

WHAT WE CALL *Oranges, Lemons, Limes, Citrons, and Grapefruits are all species of a single genus native to Asia and Melanesia. So many varieties have been developed in cultivation that names are only approximate.*

"Dioscorides classified Peaches, Apricots, Citrons, and Quinces along with the Apples because they all have the same shape. We shall speak first of what are commonly called Apples and then take up the others in order." Thus Mattioli, in a laudable effort to reduce the confusion. He makes some attempt to describe the difference between Lemons and Oranges, but it is not easy to say how close either is to the forms with which we are familiar.

The earliest known mention of any of the group is by the Arabs and, though it is not known when they were introduced into Europe, it seems a good guess that they came through Spain as various other Eastern introductions did. Certainly Oranges were imported from Spain in the seventeenth century, when they were a familiar luxury item in England and made famous the Orange girls (especially Nell Gwynn) who sold fruit in theaters. Coles says that for this reason they were known as Cevil (Seville) Oranges.

With the Oranges and the Lemons Mattioli includes what he calls Adam's Apples, which have certain indentations on the skin that the common folk believe to represent the marks of Adam's teeth. Despite the medieval tradition that Adam's Apple actually was an Apple, efforts to identify it as something else and protests that the speculation is futile went on and on. "Let us have done with such fables", says Mattioli. Half a century later, Sir Thomas Browne devotes a longish article in his Vulgar Errors *to the question. As usual, he exhibits overwhelming learning displayed in a style of gorgeous intricacy. After citing the authorities who have supported this or that candidate for the doubtful honor of tempting mankind to its fall, he writes: "Though they have received appelations suitable to the tradition, yet can we not from them infer that they were this fruit in question; no more than* Arbor vitae, *so commonly so called, to obtain its name from the tree of Life in Paradise, or* Arbor Judae, *to be the same which supplied the gibbet unto Judas."*

ORANGE

Rutaceae : Citrus

Moonwort

IN THE UNITED STATES, *this delicate little plant* (Botrychium lunaria) *is a rarity much prized by fern fanciers. There is usually only a single leaf less than ten inches long beside which grows a second stem, leafless but bearing the round spore cases which give the whole family its common name, Grape Fern. Some other members of the group are much larger and commoner, but those called Adder's-tongue most resemble* Lunaria.

Skeptical comments on the various superstitions, including those cherished by the alchemists, are especially interesting. The latter believed that Lunaria *can be made to produce pure silver, "but from them I learn how much they abuse with their fables and lies those who waste upon them all their resources and gain nothing but poverty". So remarks Mattioli.*

Despite these and other sensible comments, Culpeper was still repeating the fables nearly three-quarters of a century later: "Alchemists say that this herb is peculiarly useful to them in making silver . . . It is reported however that whatever horse casually treads upon this herb will loose its shoes . . . but whether their reports be fabulous or true, it is well known to the country people by the name of Unshoew-horse." This last fable was also well known in both Italy and France. Mattioli speaks of an herb called Sferra Cavallo and his contemporary, Guillaume du Bartas, author of the enormously popular Divine Week, *gives the same miraculous plant a prominent place among the wonders of God's creation:*

> *O Moonwort tell us where thou hid'st the Smith,*
> *Hammer and Pinchers, thou unshoest them with?*
> *Alas! what Iron Engine is't*
> *That can thy subtle secret strength resist,*
> *Sith the best Farrier cannot, set a shoe*
> *But thou (so shortly) canst undo?*

Unfortunately, both the Latin name Lunaria *and the English name Moonwort are, in the United States and England, applied also to a totally different plant, namely, a member of the Mustard family sometimes called Honesty and familiar in dried bouquets. It owes its name to those translucent, moon-shaped fruit septums which are also responsible for its decorative value.*

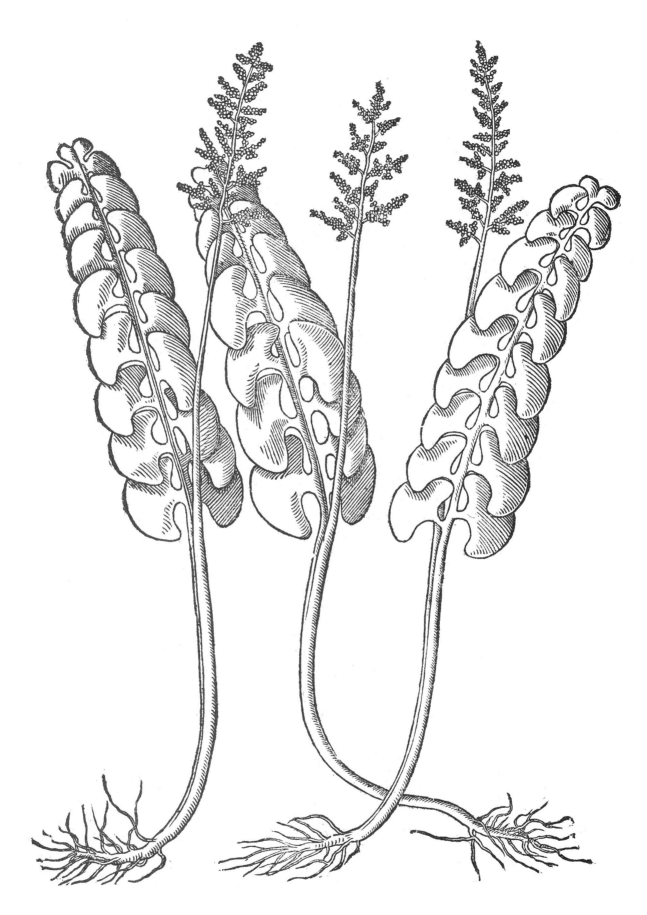

MOONWORT

Ophioglossaceae : Botrychium

Buglose

THE EARLIEST *post-classical Herbalists deferred to Dioscorides as abjectly as later medieval scholars deferred to Aristotle. Sometimes they seemed to assume that he had all the authority of that first namer of all things, Adam in the Garden of Eden. And Eden, so it was said, must have included every plant which has since grown anywhere on earth. The realization that floras varied with geography had hardly dawned upon them.*

Mattioli has, to a considerable extent, freed himself from this slavery to authority. He is well aware that the world of plants is much more extensive than Dioscorides' account of it.

His comment on the plate facing this page is a good example of his independent curiosity: "Not long ago I was brought a plant collected near Boririe . . . I have convinced myself that it conforms exactly to the description of Onosma [i.e. To one of the various species of the modern genus Onosma of the Borage family]. Therefore, I have put it here drawn from life, in order to expose it to the judgment of all . . . So far, I am not sure if this herb produces a stem, or flower, or seed, since I have never seen it except as here engraved."

This last confession of ignorance refers to Dioscorides' account of Onosma, which is mostly nonsense, from his flat statement that though the leaves are like Anchusa [another member of the Borage family] it is without stalk, flower, or seed, to his concluding remark: "They say also that if one with child go over this herb she makes abortion."

Mattioli's identification of his plant with that described by Dioscorides is probably correct and so is the present tentative identification of it as some member of that modern genus which still goes by the name Onosma. But the family is very large and a number of other close relatives were used in herbal medicine, including those belonging in the genera Anchusa and Echium.

The popular name for the Anchusas is Buglose and of the Echiums is Viper's Buglose, so called (as some of the English Herbalists tell us) because its seeds resemble a viper's head. The Hortus Sanitatis says that Anchusa "is good for him who has harmful wicked moistness of the lungs", *and Bancke's Herbal says that* "this herb drunken with hot water maketh a man to have a good mind and good wit".

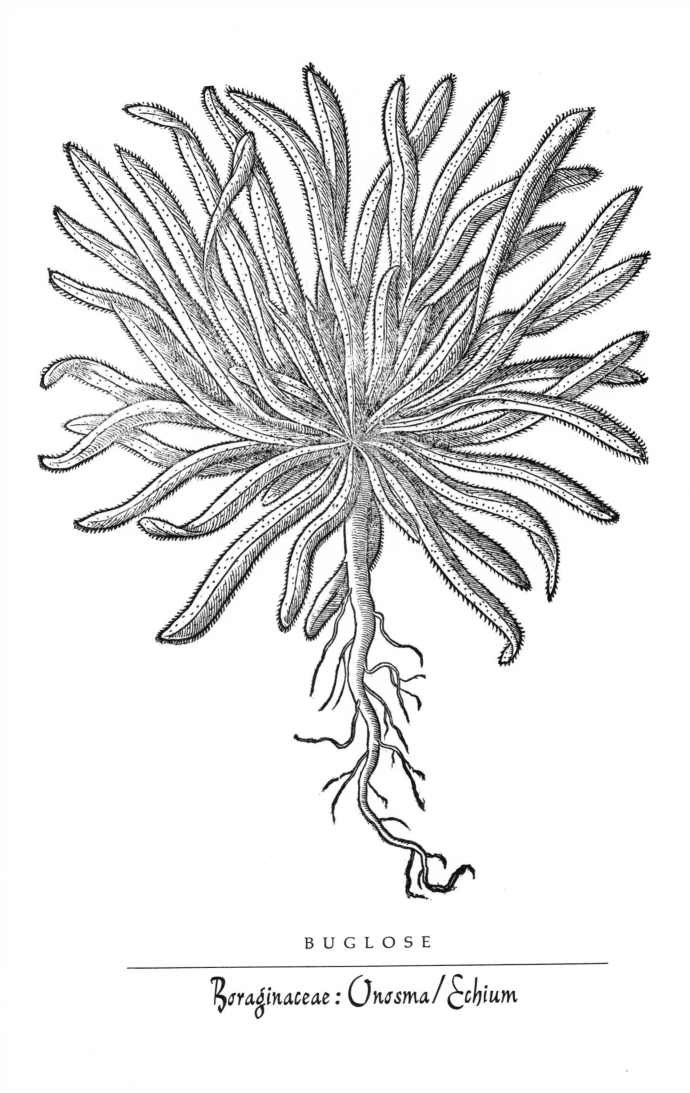

BUGLOSE

Boraginaceae: Onosma/Echium

Grape

TO THE GRAPE *and to the wines made from it, Dioscorides devotes more than one third of his last book. There are brief descriptions of two wild species of the vine, and also of what modern botany calls* Vitis vinefera, *or "the wine-giving vine". Then comes some medical advice concerning grapes and raisins, followed by a general discussion of "The Flavors of Wines and their Properties", "The Effect of Wines", and, finally, brief accounts of more than fifty table and medicated wines—ranging from those which can be made from Pears, Quinces, Pomegranates, Dates, etc. to more improbable concoctions, among which is an Abortion Wine made from grapes grown in close proximity to Hellebore or to the Wild Cucumber, and said to take on some of the characteristics of these poisonous herbs.*

Considered as a medicinal "simple" rather than as food or drink, the wild and cultivated grape are endowed with the same virtues. The leaves being beaten and mixed with porridge make a poultice which relieves headaches. The leaves are good also for snake bite and inflammation of the spleen. To drink the juice of the leaves "doth help the dysenterical, the blood spitters, and women that lust".

Both new wine and very old wine are unwholesome "but that which is of a middle age . . . is to be chosen in the uses of both health and sickness . . ." Generally all unmixed and simple wine, hard by nature, is warming, easily digested, good for the stomach, whetting the appetite, nourishing, soporiferous, inducing a good color, but being drunk liberally it helps those who have taken Hemlock, or Coriander . . . and for the biting of serpents.

"The quantity must be ordered by the age, the time of the year, and the custom of the drinker and the quality of the wine. The best rule is not to be athirst and moderately to steep meat; for all drunkenness and especially that which is continual is pernicious . . . But to be drunk moderately for some days and especially after water drinking is profitable.[!] For it alters the state of a man in a manner, purging the vapors that annoy the senses and opening the passages secretly."

Those who are shocked by what seems to them rather excessive liberality on the part of Dioscorides may be comforted by the opinion of Pliny: "It is extremely difficult to determine whether wine is more generally injurious in its effects or beneficial."

GRAPE

Vitaceae : Vitis

Hare

SOME RENAISSANCE *Herbalists followed Dioscorides in declaring that the brain of a Hare roasted and eaten is good for tremblings caused by fear—which is perhaps an example of sympathetic magic in reverse; also that the head being burned and mixed with Bear's grease will cure baldness.*

Characteristically, Mattioli adds his own bits of natural and unnatural history. Among them are three alleged facts of which two are legends and one is truth. Of the two fables, Mattioli accepts one and rejects the other. Since the three seem equally improbable a priori, they illustrate why it is so difficult to separate fact from fancy. (1) Hares sleep with open eyes because readiness for flight is their only protection against enemies. (2) Species inhabiting the mountains are white when snow covers the ground, reddish brown when it is bare. (3) All Hares are hermaphrodites. (Number 2 is the actual fact.)

HARE

Hyacinth

MATTIOLI *describes and illustrates two Hyacinths, one a common Italian native, the other "sent me from Padua by Antonio Cortusus, who writes that he received it from the Orient". He calls this second one the Oriental Hyacinthus, and it is obviously that most familiar of our garden and windowsill Hyacinths, of which the botanical name is still* H. *orientalis.*

The Oriental Hyacinth is native to Greece as well as to Asia, but it is difficult to be sure whether or not it is one of the various "Bulbs" described by Dioscorides. Mattioli, referring it would seem to the wild species, reports the belief that the root applied with white wine to young children will inhibit the growth of hair on both the face and the pubic regions. As a drink it contracts the belly, provokes urination, and is good for spider bites. The seed cures jaundice.

The Hyacinth, like the Narcissus, is the subject of one of the best known flower myths. But there is an unsolved mystery concerning the Hyacinth. The story itself, as told by Ovid, is simple enough. Apollo was passionately attached to a mortal youth named Hyacinth. They hunted and engaged in athletic sports together until one day the boy, rushing eagerly forward to follow a discus thrown by the god, was struck on the head and died. Thereupon Apollo, overcome with grief, vowed to celebrate the lost youth in song and also to create a purple flower marked Woe! Woe! (in Greek spelled Aı).

So far so good. And the poets have enthusiastically taken on Apollo's task—the best-known reference in English being probably "like to that sanguine flower inscribed with woe" in Milton's Lycidas. *But the rub is this: No flower known to us as a Hyacinth has any marking which, with the best will in the world, can possibly be interpreted as a Greek Aı. One kind used to be known as* H. noninscriptus, *but that describes them all.*

Botanists, if not the poets, have been troubled by the paradox for a long time—at least since the early seventeenth century, when an editor of Gerard moved what was called the Poet's Hyacinth from its former place and put it among the Red Lilies, because he thought the black spots on one species of Lily might be the famous "Woe! Woe!". But no one is satisfied, and attempts have been made to identify it with one or another of a long list of other flowers, including the Iris, Pansy, Larkspur, and Gladiolus.

HYACINTH

Liliaceae : Hyacinthus

Jujube

IN COMMON PARLANCE, *"Jujube" usually means today a gummy lozenge made of Gum Arabic and sugar, which is dissolved in the mouth to soothe an irritated throat. Such lozenges were, however, first so called because they were imitations of (or substitutes for) a certain dried fruit of similar consistency called by that name at least since the Renaissance. These blood red fruits, about the size of an olive, are borne on any one of several species of trees of the Buckthorn family and are most widely cultivated today in China, where they are considered a dessert delicacy.*

The Jujube illustrated here is probably closely related to that grown in China and which, according to Pliny, was first brought to Italy from Syria during the last days of the Emperor Augustus. Mattioli points out that it is not mentioned by Dioscorides, but discusses at considerable length his opinion (disputed by others) that what Galen calls Serica *is actually the Jujube. Then he quotes the following quizzical remark of the great physician: "I cannot testify concerning its properties either as a conserver of health or as a cure of disease, because the women and children have picked and eaten all of them." Avicenna, so Mattioli informs us further, holds that Jujubes are good for the stomach and lungs. Others ridicule this opinion but Mattioli supports it.*

Culpeper, as is his custom, makes very large claims and provides a prescription so complicated that it must have distracted the attention of the patient from his distress, whether or not it conferred any more substantial benefits. Here it is:

"A most valuable receipt for the cure of all sharp humors, ulcers, and inflammation in the kidneys, veins, and bladder; and for the stone, jaundice, falling sickness and dropsy . . . Take Jujube, the seed of Parsley, Fennel, Anise, and Caraway of each one ounce; of the roots of Parsley, Burnet, Saxifrage and Caraway one ounce and a half; . . . infuse them all night in a bottle of white wine and in the morning boil it in a closed earthen vessel until a third part be consumed; strain it, and drink four ounces at a time, the first and last thing morning and evening, abstaining from all other drink for at least three hours."

Jujube is said to be a corruption of the Arab name Zizowf *with which the modern generic name also is connected.*

JUJUBE

Rhamnaceae : Zizyphus

Aconite

THIS PLANT *belongs to the Buttercup family and that sounds inno-cent enough. But none ever had (and none ever deserved) a worse repu-tation. According to the Greeks, it was created by Hecate, the queen of Hell, from the froth of the three-headed dog Cereberus standing guard over her realm.*

The common name Wolfsbane is a direct translation of a Greek name, but it was evidently used to poison human beings as well. According to Theophrastus, a law prescribed the death penalty for those who so much as had it in their possession. Small doses lower the blood pressure and inhibit reflex action, but it is little used in modern medicine (nor was it, for that matter, in ancient medicine either) though its potency was so sensational that it is mentioned in English plant lists as early as the tenth century. Medea was said to have used it to poison Theseus, and the in-habitants of the Isle of Ceos included it in the beverage their old men were compelled to drink when they were no longer useful.

Bad as is the truth about Aconite, it was adorned with elaborate super-stitions. According to Theophrastus, special precautions must be ob-served when it is being gathered, but if it is taken with wine it produces no effect. It may be compounded in such a way as to produce death at a certain date—months, or even as much as years, after administration. The time it takes to kill is equal to the time which has elapsed between the collecting and the administration. The victim wastes painfully away and the longer it takes him to die the more extreme are his sufferings.

Mattioli (who is not, in general, much given to superstition) adds this: "They say that if you touch a scorpion with the root it stuns it, but that you can restore its vigor by touching it with the root of Hellebore."

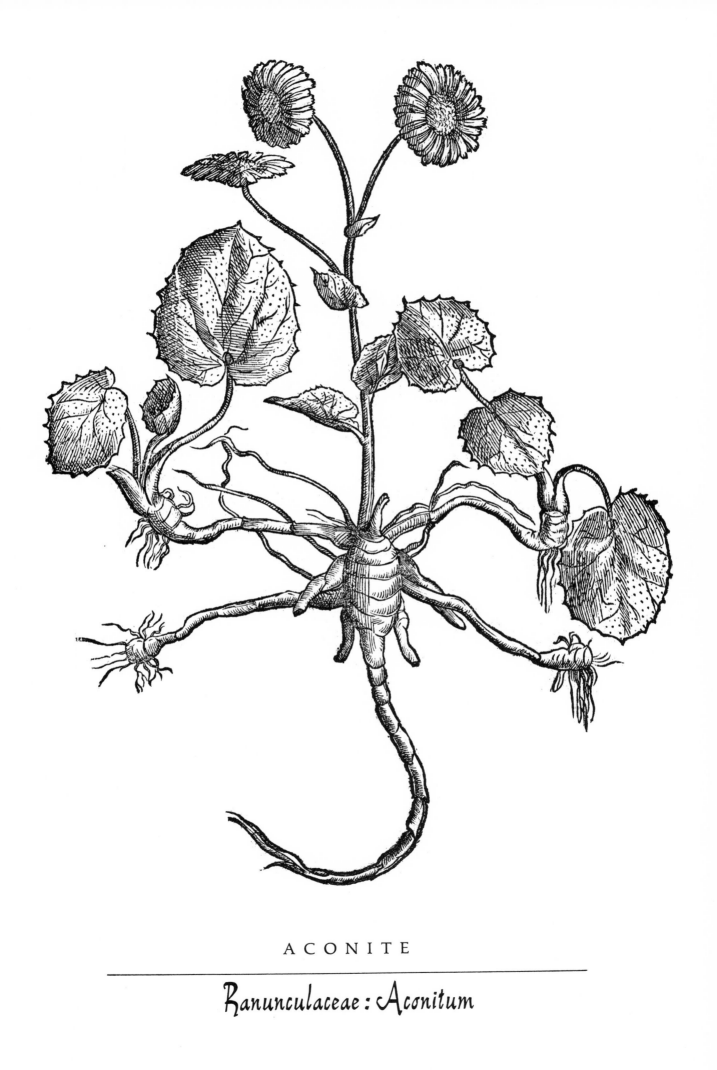

ACONITE

Ranunculaceae : Aconitum

Amaranth

IN ONE RESPECT *at least, the Amaranth is like the nightingale—more impressive in the poet's imagination than in actual fact. We in the United States know it principally as an old-fashioned garden annual* (A. caudatus) *which contributes to the winter bouquet, and as that terror of hayfever victims popularly called "Careless Weed". To the Greeks and Romans, on the other hand, the Amaranths were sacred to Artemis, symbols of immortality* (Amarantus *means "never fading"), and appropriate for garlands. Here is Pliny on what is probably the species illustrated opposite:*

"There is no doubt that all the efforts of art are surpassed by the Amaranth, which is, to speak correctly, rather a purple ear than a flower; and at the same time quite inodorous. It is a marvelous feature of this plant that it takes a delight in being gathered; indeed, the more it is plucked the better it grows. It comes into flower in the month of August and lasts throughout the autumn. The finest of all is the Amarantus of Alexander, which is generally gathered for keeping; for it is a really marvelous fact that when all the other flowers have gone out, the Amaranthus, being dipped in water, comes to life again; it is used also for making winter chaplets."

Modern poets have often borrowed the symbol, though none pushes it further than Milton:

> *Immortal Amaranth, a flower that once*
> *In Paradise, fast by the Tree of Life*
> *Began to bloom, but soon for man's offence*
> *To heaven removed, where first it grew, there grows,*
> *And flowers aloft shading the Font of Life.*
>
> PARADISE LOST. BOOK III

As a garden flower, various species and varieties seem to have been popular in Shakespeare's time when Gerard (who was as much gardener as Herbalist) speaks glowingly of a species with colored foliage, and also of what his illustration plainly reveals to be our Cockscomb. The former he calls Floramor (Amarantus tricolor) *and exclaims: "Every leaf resembleth in color the most fair and beautiful feather of a parrot . . . Nature hath bestowed her greatest jollity upon this flower."*

A M A R A N T H

Amarantaceae : Amarantus

Ethiopian Pepper

OF THE VARIOUS SPICES *and condiments known to Greece and Rome, the most usual was the true Pepper* (Piper nigrum), *which had long been imported from the East. It was valued so highly that the ransom demanded by Alaric after the sack of Rome was paid partly in Pepper. During the sixteenth century the price rose so high that it inspired the Portuguese to search out the Cape of Good Hope route to the Orient, after Columbus' quest for "the Indies" had failed to reach the real Indies where the spices were to be found. Columbus, to be sure, thought that he had found Pepper in the West Indies when he discovered what looked like peppercorns, but they turned out to be Allspice—which seems to be the only spice (if you don't count Red and Green Peppers) found in the Western Hemisphere.*

The difference between white and black Pepper is the result of the method used in curing the berries of the same plant, but as late as 1525 the anonymous Herbal printed in England could report with a straight face: "Some say that Pepper is made black with burning in the fire, for when it is gathered there be great multitudes of serpents about and therefore they put it in the fire to burn the serpents that be about it."

True Pepper was the one best known (and not too well at that) to Dioscorides, whose longish treatment of it contains a number of statements of the sort almost inevitable when the actual source of a familiar product is known only at second hand. Mattioli corrects most of these errors because, as he is glad to acknowledge, the Portuguese and the Spaniards have explored regions of the earth unknown to the classical geographers and brought back "not only Pepper but also Truth".

What he calls Ethiopian Pepper (Xylopia aethiopia), *and is accurately illustrated in his book, is a member of the Custard Apple family, which includes such other tropical fruits as the Soursop and the Cherimoya. It is native to West Africa; was long brought by caravans across the Sahara to the Mediterranean regions; and was probably used by the Romans, though not distinguished by them from the true Pepper. (How many present day users of Pepper know what kind of vine it comes from?) In Africa, the beans of the Ethiopian Pepper are so valued they are said to be used sometimes as money.*

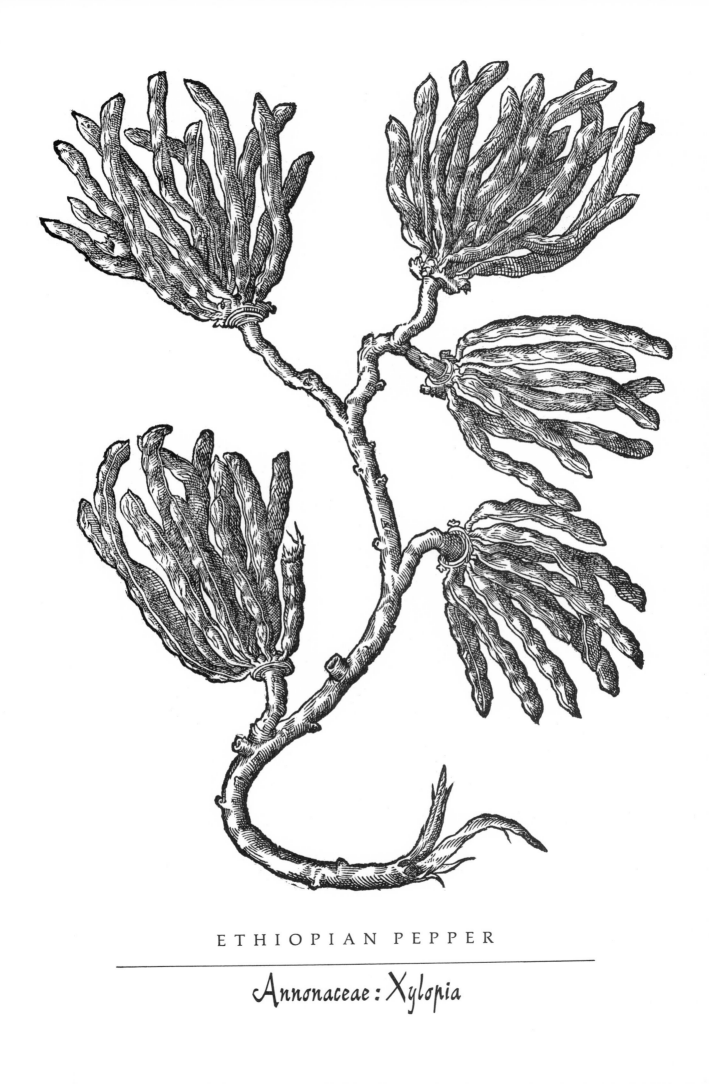

ETHIOPIAN PEPPER

Annonaceae : Xylopia

Burreed

IN MOST CASES, *the virtues attributed by any of the Herbalists to their "simples" are bewilderingly diverse and numerous. In the case of this familiar weed of the pondside, Dioscorides is, however, unaccustomedly brief. So far as medicine is concerned, he disposes of it in a single sentence. "The root and seed taken in wine is good against the bite of serpents."*

Perhaps this disinclination to dwell on Sparganium *was due in part to the fact that (as in the case of the Bulrush, or Cattail) neither he nor the renaissance Herbalists knew quite what to make of it or in what company to put it. And in both cases their difficulty was the same: they had no significant criteria for grouping their specimens. Sometimes they hit upon some obvious characteristic—like, for instance, the presence of thorns—and on that basis threw together species which actually were related and others which were, in more fundamental characteristics, far apart. Such was the case, for example, when they put Woodsorrel* (Oxalis) *with the Clovers just because it had three leaflets to a stem. Thus Mattioli, following Dioscorides, puts the Burreed between a Gladiolus and an Iris simply because it has, like them, sword-shaped leaves.*

The Gladiolus and Iris actually do belong in the same family. But the Burreed is a very strange bedfellow to put between them, and Mattioli's brief description makes it clear how little except leaf shape it has in common with either the Gladiolus or the Iris. "It has", he writes, "leaves like those of the Gladiolus but narrower and bending more toward the earth. At the summit of the stem it produces certain balls composed of seed crowded together".

Almost two hundred years were to pass before Linneaus brought order out of chaos by sensing that the structure of the flower affords the most significant single clue to plant relationships. Accept that fact and it becomes immediately evident that the Burreed belongs close to the Cattail (see page 106). Like the latter it has a very primitive, but not identical, floral structure. Modern classification puts it in a family of its own but close to the Cattail.

Despite the popular name, the Burreed is not a Reed. The latter, unlike the Burreed and like all the other members of the grass family to which it belongs, has a stem closed at the nodes.

BURREED

Sparganiaceae : Sparganium

Saxifrage

T H E   S A X I F R A G E S *include some four hundred species of this genus alone, many of them well-known rock garden plants. Both the popular and the botanical names are from the Latin (which means rock breaker) and have been variously explained; sometimes as referring to the fact that some species grow among rocks, more often because they were supposed to break up kidney stones. Whichever explanation came first, it probably influenced the other, and those species which grow among broken rocks were supposed to provide thus a "signature" indicative of their use.*

Mattioli discusses several species, and says that they "suppress hiccups, break up stones, and produce ready urination". Mostly, however, he is concerned with the question of identification and with his reason for suspecting that the chapter devoted to the Saxifrages in most editions of Dioscorides is an addition, not part of his original work; also to the fact that various other, quite different plants, are called Saxifrage because they are supposed to have similar medicinal virtues. Among them is what he calls Pimpinella, *now that genus of the Carrot family which includes also the Anise* (P. Anisum) *familiar as a food spice.*

Culpeper writes: "There are not many better medicines to break the stone than this, or to cleanse the urinary passages and cure the gravel." Gerard also discusses at great length the problem of identity.

The name, he says, has in late years been imposed upon a number of plants differing among themselves in shape and place of growth, and agreeing only in the fact that they have the power of expelling kidney stones. "I think it not amiss a little to enquire whether Saxifrage was known to the ancients, and if known to what kind it may probably be referred".

As for the Pimpinellas, *he treats two species, of which the one he calls* P. saxifraga *is obviously of the Carrot family* (Umbelliferae). *"Some make also a great case for it as a protection against the plague."*

SAXIFRAGE

Saxifragaceae : Saxifraga

Buckthorn

THE BUCKTHORNS *are spiny shrubs of which there are many species both in Europe and the United States. Dioscorides mentions three sorts and Mattioli attempts to distinguish between them. Fortunately, however, all three have (according to him) the same virtue: they are an excellent remedy for eczema and erysipelas. Then, with a cautious "they say", he follows Dioscorides in reporting that "the branches of Rhamnus when put at the doors and windows of houses drive away all enchantments and sorceries". John Goodyear, seventeenth-century translater of Dioscorides, adds that "if any take up Rhamnus, the moon decreasing, and bear it, it is profitable against poison and against naughty men, and it is good for beasts to bear about them and to be put about ships, and is good against the pain of the head, and against devils and their assaults". It was also one of the many thorny shrubs or trees sometimes supposed to have composed Christ's crown at the crucifixion.*

Dioscorides makes no mention of the genuine medicinal properties of most of the Buckthorns, but they were recognized at least as early as the sixteenth century, when the Herbalist Dodoens somewhat snobbishily commented upon their cathartic properties in these words: "They [Buckthorn berries] are not meet to be administered but to young and lusty people of the country, which do set more store by their money than their lives."

Actually, however, a species from the West Coast of the United States supplies the bark from which cascara sagrada is extracted, and in England the berries collected from wild plants are said to have been a favorite among country people as a purgative for children as late as the nineteenth century. Buckthorn first appeared in the London Pharmocopoeia in 1650, where it was the active ingredient in a mixture which included also Anise seed, Cinnamon, Mastic, and Nutmeg. It ceased to be an official British medicine during the second half of the nineteenth century, but is said to be still commonly prescribed by veterinarians in conjunction with castor oil.

Pliny (whose identification is somewhat dubious) says that the root of Rhamnus is boiled in water to make a medicine known as Lycian, and that the seed "is useful for bringing away the afterbirth".

BUCKTHORN

Fowl

FROM CLASSICAL TIMES *to the present, physicians have recommended Chicken broth and soft-boiled eggs for the ailing, but fortunately they no longer treat snake bite by applying the opened carcasses of fresh-killed fowls—which must be changed often. A more interesting quasi-medical use is alluded to in the twelfth-century Ms already quoted à propos the Deer (see page 52):*

"Cockcrow is a pleasant thing of a night, and not only pleasant but useful . . . It wakes the sleeping, it forewarns the anxious, it consoles the traveller . . . At his crowing the devoted mind rises in prayer and the priest begins again to read his office. By testifying devotedly after cockcrow Peter washed away the sin of the Church, which he had incurred by denying Christ before it crowed. It is by his song that hope returns to the sick, trouble is turned to advantage, the pain of wounds is relieved, the burning of fever is lessened, faith is restored to the fallen, Christ turns His face to the wavering, or reforms the erring; wandering of mind departs and negation is driven out."

Mattioli is less eloquent but he repeats a strange tale: Cocks will not crow if a segment of vine is tied around their necks.

FOWL

Nutmeg

140

OF ALL *the lying travelers who have ever written books, the most outrageous was that fourteenth-century faker who called himself Sir John Mandeville. Just where he cribbed his statement that Mace and Nutmeg come from the same tree is not known—but for once it happens to be a true statement. The Nutmeg is the hard seed and Mace one of the seed coatings produced by an evergreen tree native to the Moluccas, or Spice Islands. Both were unknown to Europe until they are said to have been introduced in the twelfth century, and they must have been very rare until the Moluccas were discovered by the Dutch in the sixteenth. The many early literary references show how soon they became standard delicacies, perhaps especially in spiced drinks:*

> *Nutmegs and Ginger, Cinnamon and Cloves,*
> *And they gave me this jolly red nose.*

So sings a character in Beaumont and Fletcher's Knight of the Burning Pestle, *while the clown in* The Winter's Tale *reads a list of the needs to prepare a shepherd's feast:* "I must have Saffron to color the warden [Pear] pies; Mace, Dates—none, that's out of my note; Nutmegs, seven; a race or two of Ginger, but that I may beg; four pound of Prunes, and as many o' raisins o' the sun." *Yet, Nutmegs must have remained costly enough to inspire early Connecticut's most famous industry. As Thomas Hamilton wrote in his* Men and Manners in America: "Yankee peddlers . . . always have a large assortment of wooden Nutmegs and stagnant barometers."

Though both Nutmegs and Mace have pretty well disappeared from medicine except as flavorings and as a mild carminative, they once had a great reputation. The reticulated surface of the Nutmeg constituted a plain "signature" indicating that it was good for the brain; but it was most famous as affording protection against infection during epidemics of the plague. G. W. Piesse's The Art of Perfumery *gives instructions for preparing the "Vinegar of the Four Thieves", said to have been used by thieves to protect themselves while robbing corpses during the Marseille plague of 1722.*

A pleasanter association is the fact that it was once common to give a gilded Nutmeg at Christmas:

> *I had a little nut tree, nothing would it bear*
> *But a silver nutmeg and a golden pear.*

NUTMEG

Myristicaceae : Myristica

Yew

THE YEW TREE, *like the Date Palm, is one of the relatively few plants which are called by botanists dioecious—which means having separate male and female flowers borne on separate plants. It is also so well known as a rather formal glossy-leaved ornamental that (as the Herbalists sometimes say of a very familiar plant) it is not necessary to describe it. Of course, only the female plants produce the attractive berries.*

No doubt because of its somber darkness, the Yew has long been associated with witchcraft, churchyards, and mourning. In the tenth-century Anglo-Saxon Leech Book *it is recommended for use in connection with a charm against "the water elf disease", and it is one of the ingredients of the witches' brew in* Macbeth. *It also appears as a symbol of death or mourning in many English plays and poems,. as, for instance, "My shroud of white stuck all with Yew" (Twelfth Night) and "Strew on her roses, roses/ And never a sprig of Yew/ In quiet she reposes/ Ah! would that I did too" (Matthew Arnold).*

In ancient times, the chief practical use of the Yew resulted from its extremely tough texture. It was the preferred wood for the famous English longbow, and the American Indians of the Northwest Coast used a related species for bows, spear handles, canoe paddles, fishhooks, and fence posts.

From classical times to the present, botanists have disputed which parts of the tree are poisonous and to what extent. Dioscorides reports that those which grow in a certain part of what is now France are said to be so dangerous that they are sometimes fatal to those who merely rest under them. Pliny dutifully repeats this and declares also that wine vessels made of the wood have been the cause of death. Then he adds, "it has been discovered that these poisonous qualities are quite neutralized by driving a copper nail into the wood of the tree".

Modern opinion seems to be that the seeds of the berries are probably poisonous but that the flesh is not; also that at least the young branches may be dangerous to animals that eat them.

YEW

Taxaceae : Taxus

Goatsbeard

THERE ARE *at least thirty-five species of the genus* Tragopogon, *several of which are common weeds in the United States. The English common name translates the ancient Greek and refers to the tuft of plumes with which the air-borne seeds are, like those of the dandelion and some other members of the* Composite *family, abundantly provided.*

Rather unexpectedly, one member of the genus, Tragopogon porrifolius, *is the edible Salsify, or Oysterplant. It also is sufficiently weedlike to have escaped in parts of the United States and it is apparently the species to which both Dioscorides and Mattioli refer, though the latter gives it a much fuller treatment and mentions also another species.*

"The Goatsbeard is sufficiently well known. In winter, the root is eaten as a salad because it is sweet. . . . Its flower is yellow and somewhat like that of the Dandelion, though larger and enclosed in a sort of button. When the weather is clear it remains wide open; when it is cloudy the flower closes up in its button . . . From the top of the button hangs a frolicsome beard which is white and rather large and which is, according to Theophrastus, the reason why this herb is called Goatsbeard.

"The juice or the liquid distilled in an alembic and applied with a linen swab or pad to fresh or bleeding sores will make them close and form scars. . . . There is another sort of Goatsbeard which is called Purpurin because of its purplish leaves. It bears at its summit flowers which are purple and smaller and branch out in star-like formation. Its root is large and thick and full of a bitter and biting milk, not sweet like the other."

For some reason, Pliny makes much wider claims for the medicinal value of the Goatsbeard, listing seventeen applications of which the oddest is this: "Mixed with woman's milk it is a cure for all diseases of the eye . . . and dimness of the sight more particularly." Culpeper places it under the dominion of Saturn and says that it is "cooling, somewhat dry and binding, and therefore good for the heat and gnawings of the stomach".

GOATSBEARD

Compositae : Tragopogon

Rose

VARIOUS SINGLE ROSES *are native to the Mediterranean region, but just when and how the innumerable double kinds were introduced (probably from Asia) it is impossible to say. They do not appear as a motive in Egyptian art, and what is called "Rose" in the English Bible is almost certainly something else. One does figure in a fresco in the palace of King Minos, but neither Homer's "Rosy fingered dawn" nor the many references in later Greek poets help much. On the other hand, Pompeian frescos show what appears to be a Damask Rose. Pliny says there are twenty-five varieties.*

In any case, and from Roman times to the present day, no flower has been so often referred to. It was a symbol of Venus, of Dionysus, of Bacchus, and later of the Virgin Mary also. Nero is said to have spent the equivalent of 150,000 dollars to supply a single banquet with the Roses traditionally scattered at a certain crucial moment, and the custom of doing so affords one of the various explanations of "sub rosa". After the roses were scattered all happenings were to be kept secret.

During the Middle Ages, the Rose was a symbol of the Mystic Vision, of Courtly Love, and also of the female pudenda. In the Book of Secrets *we are told that a gram of the flower, a mustard seed, and the foot of a weasel hung in a tree will prevent its bearing fruit. More sensible uses of it were made by medieval ladies who washed their hands in rosewater, sprinkled Rose leaves in clothes chests, and ate Rosepetal candy.*

Perhaps the best-known encomium is that of Gerard: "The plant of Roses, though it be a shrub full of prickles, yet it had been more fit and convenient to have placed it with the most gorgeous flowers of the world than to insert the same here among base and thorny shrubs: for the Rose doth deserve the chieftest and prime place among all the flowers whatsoever; being not only esteemed for his beauty, virtues and his fragrant and odoriferous smell; but also because it is the honor and ornament of our English scepter . . . in uniting of those two most Royal Houses of Lancaster and York."

From this it is something of a letdown to read Gerard's prosy account of the not very spectacular medicinal virtues of the queen of flowers. The distilled water of Roses, he says, is good for the heart and refreshes the spirits; Roses also give a delightful taste to "junketting dishes", cakes, sauces, and other pleasant things.

ROSE

Rosaceae : Rosa

Henbane

A RECENT ARTICLE *in a medical journal raises again an old question: Of what poison did Hamlet's father die?*

According to the tale told by his Ghost:

> *Upon my secure hour thy uncle stole,*
> *With juice of cursed hebenon in a vial,*
> *And in the porches of my ears did pour*
> *The leprous distillment.*

But what was this "hebenon" which does not appear in any contemporary Herbal? Was it Henbane, Ebony, or an extract of the English Yew called "hebon" by Marlow and other Elizabethans? Would any of them serve as a sudden and fatal poison if poured into an ear? Perhaps not, but the Herbals recommend that various medications (one for toothache) be administered in that strange way and Pliny, in his discussion of Henbane, says: "From the seed an oil is extracted which injected into the ears, deranges the intellect."

Dioscorides distinguishes three species of this poisonous relative of the Tomato: the White, the Yellow, and the Black, of which the last, the Hyoscyamus niger of modern botany, is the most virulent. It is native to the Mediterranean region but has become naturalized in parts of the United States. Modern medicine sometimes uses it or its active principle, which is closely related to atropine. It is an anodyne but can bring on hallucinations and death.

In Greek mythology, the shades of the dead were crowned with Henbane as they wandered hopeless beside the Styx, and its dangerous effects were well known. Dioscorides calls the Black and Yellow Henbanes "causers of frenzies and sleep" and "scarce usable".

Perhaps the most curious use is reported by Gerard: "The seed is used by mountebank tooth-drawers which run about the country to cause worms come forth of the teeth, by burning it in a chafing dish of coals, the party holding his mouth over the fumes thereof." No doubt these fumes had an anesthetic effect, but the mountebanks had another trick to impress their customers. "Some crafty companions to gain money convey small lute strings into the water, persuading the patient that these small creepers came out of his mouth or other parts which he intended to ease." Anthropologists report similar tricks played by the medicine men of various tribes.

HENBANE

Solanaceae : Hyoscyamus

Rice

OUR CULTIVATED RICE (Oryza sativa) *is generally supposed to be descended from a wild species native to Asia, which is by some botanists given the same specific name as the cultivated. The history of its spread over the Orient, the Near East and, finally, Europe, is so complicated and so obscure that it best be left to the experts, though its names in various languages are revealing: Greek, Oruza; Latin, Oryza; Spanish, Aroz; Italian, Riso; French, Riz; and English, Rice.*

"Oruza", says Dioscorides, "is a kind of corn growing in marshy and moist places, moderately nourishing and binding to the belly". That is good enough as far as it goes, but it doesn't go very far. Add the fact that Rice is not mentioned in the Old Testament but is in the Talmud and you have one of several bits of evidence which point to the conclusion that it was slowly moving westward.

According to Mattioli, Galen (roughly a century after Dioscorides) has a good deal more to say about it than Dioscorides had. The Arabs are said to have carried it into Spain and (again according to Mattioli) it was in his time flourishing in marshy regions of Italy. He says also that it is much eaten; very easy of digestion; and of excellent flavor, especially if cooked with milk. It is of great aid to those suffering from dysentery and "some affirm that, if mixed with sugar and cinnamon, it makes one skilful in his relation with the ladies".

At about the same time, Rice was a familiar food in England, though Gerard says he was unable to make it flower in his garden and that it is usually imported from Spain already "purged and prepared after the manner of French Barley. In England we use it to make with milk a certain food or pottage . . . Many other good kinds of food are made with this kind of grain as those that are skilful in cooking can tell".

Probably the first mention of what we now think of as Japanese saki occurs in Marco Polo's thirteenth-century Travels: *"The greater part of the inhabitants of the Province of Cathay drink a sort of wine mixed with a variety of spices and drugs. This beverage . . . is so good and well flavored that they do not wish for a better. It is clear, bright and pleasant to the taste, and being made very hot, has the quality of inebriating sooner than any other."*

RICE

Gramineae: Oryza

Iris

THE GLADWIN, *or Stinking, Iris* (Iris foetidissima) *is one of the two members of the Iris family which grows wild in Great Britain as well as in southern Europe and North Africa. Its flowers are of a dull, leaden blue in color, and the unpleasant odor which any part of the plant gives off when crushed is responsible for various uncomplimentary popular names—also, perhaps [on the theory that what smells or tastes bad is probably good for you], for the fact that the Herbalists are more concerned with it than with any of the more attractive Irises.*

Several species of the genus were well known to the ancients, including Pliny, who does not attempt to distinguish among them, but remarks that the roots are widely used in both perfumes and medicine. Dioscorides singles out Iris foetidissima: *"The root with many joints, long, red, being good for wounds in the head and fractures. It draws out prickles and all sorts of weapons without pain." It also cures all swellings and inflammations and, in mixtures, various other disorders.*

Gerard says that in England it is grown in many gardens but may also be found in the wild state. "I have seen it wild in many places, as in woods and shadowy places near the sea." Culpeper also refers to it as found in England both wild and in gardens. He calls it under the dominion of Saturn, and says that if administered as a pessary it "causeth abortion in women with child".

Theophrastus recommends an Iris ointment as good against scrofula, and Pliny cites him as authority for a curious superstition: "Persons intent upon taking up the Iris drench the ground around it some three months with Hydromel, as though this were a sort of atonement offered to appease the earth; also, they trace three circles around it with the point of a sword, and the moment it is gathered they lift it up towards heaven." [According to Dioscorides, Hydromel is a sort of Quince wine fermented in sunlight during the Dog Days.]

Iris *was the Greek name of the plant, no doubt in reference to the nymph Iris, who personified the rainbow and appears in the Iliad as a messenger from the gods to men. According to the Oxford Dictionary, iris, with the meaning "rainbow", first appears in English in 1480 and as the colored portion of the eye first in 1525.*

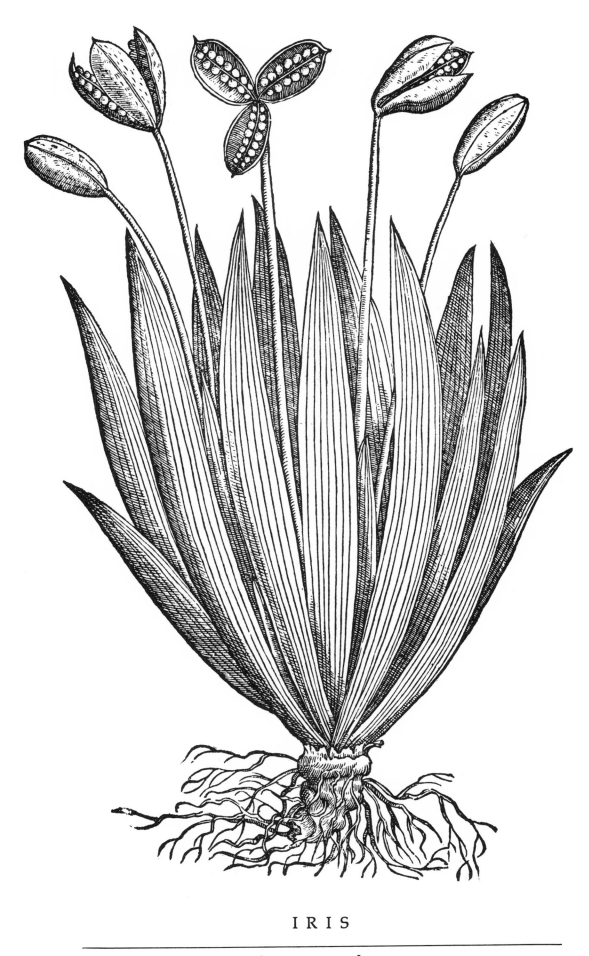

IRIS

Iridaceae : Iris

Asparagus

MODERN BOTANY *recognizes about one hundred fifty species of the genus* Asparagus, *but only two are of much interest—*A. officinalis, *the cultivated vegetable, and* A. plumosus, *of which several different varieties are cultivated by florists as a decorative green.*

Various species are native over a wide area including the Mediterranean region but Dioscorides, being interested only in medicinal uses, mentions only one and it is presumably this wild herb that Mattioli illustrates. The latter does, however, refer to the cultivated Asparagus also and so, for that matter, do some of the old Greek and Latin writers. "The cultivated kinds", says Mattioli, "are found everywhere in gardens and are so common that it would be rather foolish to amuse oneself by describing them"—which foolish amusement he proceeds to indulge in.

He notes that cooked Asparagus shoots provoke urination and that a decoction of the root is good for those who have jaundice, sciatica, pain in the kidneys or difficulty in urination. Cooked in wine, the roots are good also for insect bites and, if held in the mouth, will relieve toothache. "They say [which is Mattioli's formula when he does not want to omit anything found in an authority but also doesn't want to assume responsibility for it] that dogs will die if they drink this concoction. They say, also, that ram's horns, powdered and buried, will produce asparagus but that, according to my judgment, is completely contrary to truth."

Unlike us moderns, Mattioli does not seem to regard Asparagus as an especial delicacy among vegetables though he does say that the young shoots are more nourishing than other pot herbs and that the cultivated species seem to have much the same virtues as the wild. From ancient writers not mentioned in Dioscorides, he adds a few tidbits. According to Pliny, Asparagus, eaten frequently, improves the eyesight and inclines to "luxury". Avicenna (the Arabian physician) says that those who nourish themselves on Asparagus will feel good throughout all their bodies, despite the fact that their urine will have a very bad odor.

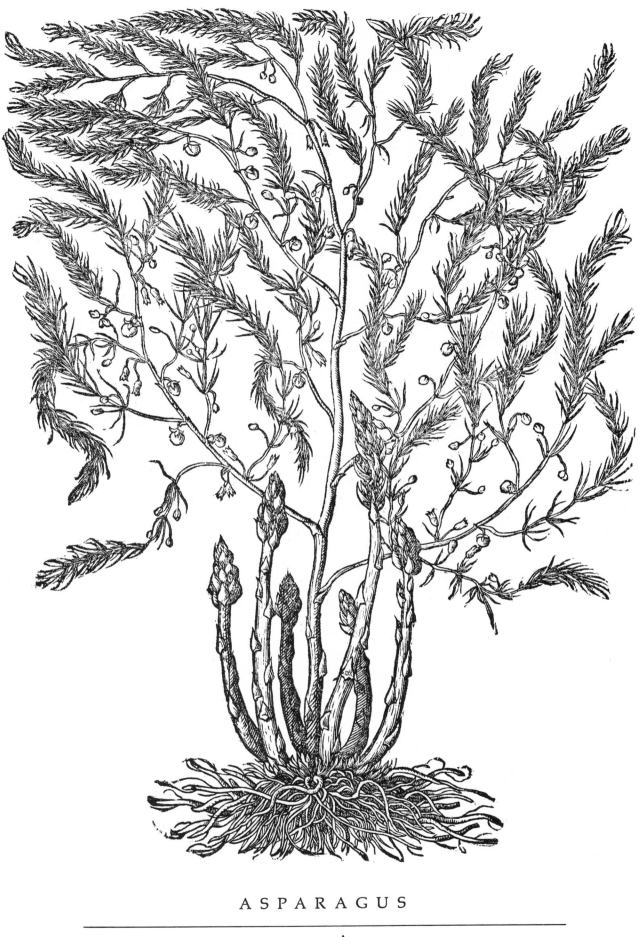

ASPARAGUS

Liliaceae : Asparagus

Black Hellebore

THREE PLANT FAMILIES *supplied the four classic poisons: Hemlock, Nightshade, Aconite, and Hellebore. The two last are members of the Buttercup family and all but the first still have at least minor medicinal uses. The active principle of H. niger appears in the U.S. Dispensary as a heart stimulant, and the plant itself is grown in gardens where it is known as the Christmas Rose because of its habit of blooming in midwinter. All varieties are natives of Europe, Asia, or both and, though there is some doubt as to which of the modern species they should be referred, we may adopt the Herbalists' designations: White Hellebore and Black.*

The sinister fascination exercised by the known virulence of Hellebore's poison is no doubt responsible for the fact that a whole mythology as well as an elaborate set of superstitions gathered around it. Pliny and others explain the name Melapodion, *applied in ancient Greece to one of the species, by saying that Melapus, the earliest of the physicians and soothsayers, observed that goats browsing upon Hellebore were violently purged. With the milk of these goats he cured the daughters of Proteus who had been afflicted with madness as a punishment for their refusal to worship Dionysus.*

He adds that Black Hellebore is gathered with more numerous ceremonies than are observed in the collection of any other plant. A circle is first drawn around it with a sword. Then the person about to cut it turns toward the East and offers up a prayer, entreating permission of the gods to collect it. At the same time, he observes whether or not an eagle is in sight, because the close approach of a bird presages the death of the collector within the year.

"The White also", he continues, "is gathered not without difficulty as it is very oppressive to the head; more especially if the precaution has not been used of eating garlic first and of drinking wine now and then, care being also taken to dig up the plant as speedily as possible".

Theophrastus indicates that one may become immune by taking Hellebore and other poisons frequently in small doses, and says that a certain druggist named Edemus once drank twenty-two draughts of Hellebore in one day without suffering an evil consequence, though he is believed to have taken an antidote at the same time.

BLACK HELLEBORE

Ranunculaceae: Helleborus

White Hellebore

"IN FORMER DAYS", *says Pliny, "Hellebore was regarded with horror, but more recently the use of it has become so familiar that numbers of studious men are in the habit of taking it for the purpose of sharpening the intellectual powers . . . Carnedas for instance made use of it when about to answer the treatises of Zeno".*

Of the Black Hellebore Dioscorides says: "It is good for the epileptic, melancholic, arthritic, and paralyzed. Given in a pessary it expels the menses and kills the embryo. Being put in fistulas and left for three days it cures them. Similarly, it is put into the ear of those who are hard of hearing and left there for two or three days. Being laid on with vinegar it heals impetigo and leprosies. Boiled with vinegar and used as a mouthwash it relieves toothaches."

Many of the same virtues are attributed to the White Hellebore. In addition, however, it is said by Dioscorides to provoke sneezing and, if mixed with honey, to kill mice. When administered to human beings it is usually either given with much juice or after a small amount of food. It purges without danger if so given. "Suppositories, if put into the seat with vinegar, provoke vomitings."

Theophrastus ridicules most of the superstitions concerning the precautions to be taken in gathering the various herbs, but considers it quite possible that the poison of Hellebore is sufficiently powerful to cause giddiness in those who gather it.

Perhaps because at least one species of Hellebore is native in the British Isles superstitions connected with it lingered long. Gilbert White, in his Natural History of Selborn, *describes some of them, and both Parkinson and Culpeper remark on the fact that rustics use it in the practice of a harmless sort of magic. "Country people use it for the cure of such beasts as are troubled with the cough or have taken any poison, by boring a hole through the ear and putting a piece of the root therein; this they say will give relief in twenty-four hours time" (Culpeper).*

Use as a vermifuge continued in England at least into the eighteenth century, though the following warning was given in a magazine article at that time: "Where it killed not the patient it would certainly kill the worms, but the worst of it is that it will sometimes kill both."

WHITE HELLEBORE

Ranunculaceae: Helleborus

Sea Holly

MEMBERS OF THIS GENUS *of the Carrot family are grown as borders or in rock gardens for the sake of their usually blue flowers and handsome spiny leaves. To the Herbalists they had various extremely valuable medicinal properties, especially for that art of giving comfort to the aged which we now call so grandly Geriatrics.*

"The roots", says Gerard, "conditioned or preserved with sugar . . . are exceeding good to give to old people that are consumed and withered with age . . . They are also good for other sorts of people that have no delight or appetite to venery, nourishing and amending the defects of nature in the younger".

He then gives elaborate directions for making a confection, in which form the remedy is most pleasant. He repeats Plutarch's story that if one sheep in a flock takes a leaf of Sea Holly in her mouth, she, and then the whole flock, will stand still until the shepherd takes the leaf out of the first sheep's mouth.

Gerard mentions only in passing that this herb is an aphrodisiac, but Coles puts it high on his list of thirteen plants useful "for provoking lust". He says also that it is a remedy for the "French pox", though without remarking how fortunate under the circumstances this is.

All the Herbalists, and more especially the classical writers, were very much interested in aphrodisiacs (moderns of course are not) and recommended a most astonishing variety of plant and animal substances, including, especially, certain Orchids for which the usual name was Satyrium. Pliny observes that the statements made by Theophrastus (an author of high authority) are really incredible: "For instance he says that by contact only of a certain plant a man has been enabled .in sexual congress to repeat his embraces as many as seventy times. The name and genus of this plant he has, however, omitted to mention."(!)

Pliny describes various ointments but expresses some skepticism concerning the belief that if the ashes of a spotted lizard are placed in linen and held in the left hand they will act as an aphrodisiac, while if held in the right they will have a contrary effect. Candied root of the Sea Holly seems the pleasantest of these prescriptions and is probably no less effective than the best of the others.

SEA HOLLY

Umbelliferae : Eryngium

Indian Corn

INDIAN CORN *seems to have been unknown to the ancients even as a rumor. Columbus himself is said to have carried it to Spain, but more than a century later it was, in England, still curiosity enough to be a prize specimen in Gerard's London garden.*

Mattioli describes the plant carefully; gives an account of the Indians' method of planting it; and recommends it as a poultice more warmly than as a food, because it is the occasion of "obstructions". Gerard calls it "Turkey Corn" since that was, apparently, the usual English name, but he is careful to point out its inaccuracy. "These kinds of grain were first brought into Spain and then into other provinces of Europe not (as some suppose) out of Asia Minor . . . but out of America and the islands adjoining . . . where they use to sow or set it to make bread . . . It is of sundry colors sometimes red and sometimes yellow, as I myself have seen in mine own garden where it hath come to ripeness."

Botanically, Maize is a member of the grass family with monstrously enlarged seeds. For once the archeologists rather than the paleontologists throw most of such light as we have on its history. It grows wild in no form remotely resembling the cultivated species, all the varieties of which are known as Zea maize. *Thumb-sized ears have been found in ancient Indian caves and they must have grown gradually larger over the centuries. It is generally supposed that several different wild genera were involved in repeated hybridizations.*

The "tassel" is a group of male flowers; the "silk" a collection of stigmas each attached to an ovary. James Logan, the Quaker provincial governor of Pennsylvania, contributed importantly to the growing understanding of plant sexuality by demonstrating that Maize would set no grain if all the tassels in a plantation were removed.

Europeans have never regarded Maize as more than a faute de mieux *food. Gerard makes it evident that this prejudice goes back to the first introduction of the unfamiliar grain. He calls it hard to digest, less nourishing than wheat, rice, barley, or oats and, in fact, hardly nourishing at all. "The barbarous Indians who know no better are constrained to make a virtue of necessity and think it good food, whereas we may easily judge [it] . . . a more convenient food for swine than for man."*

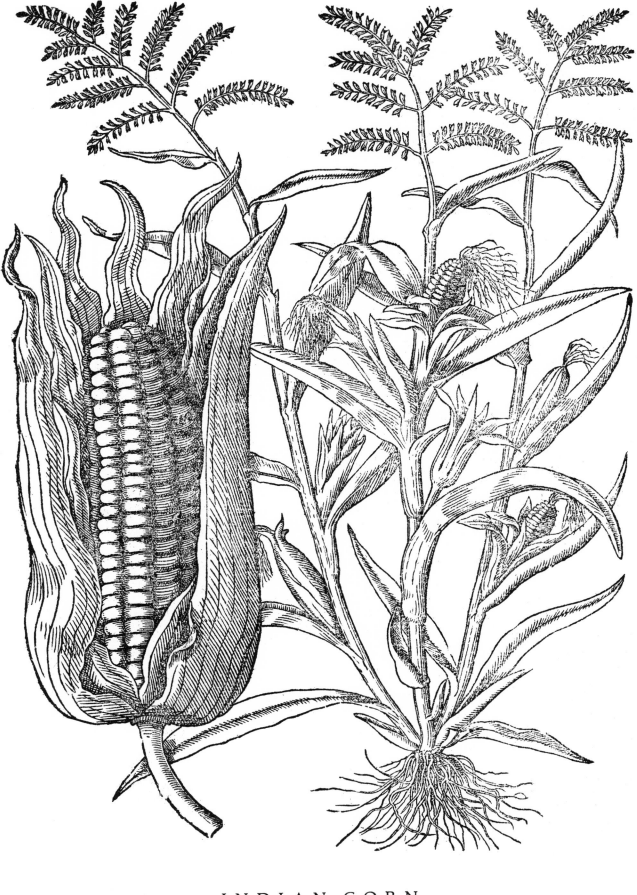

INDIAN CORN

Gramineae : Zea

Hypocistus

THE NAME *Hypocistus has fallen completely out of use, though it is obviously intended to mean "on Cistus", Cistus being still the modern name for members of the Rockrose family. The illustration makes it evident that the plant so named by Mattioli is one of the root parasites popularly called Broomrapes* (Orobanche).

He was familiar with the Broomrapes because he treats other very similar species. In fact, he says that the flowers "recall" those of the Orobanches, yet goes on to describe the plant almost as though it were a species of Cistus, despite the following ambiguous statement: "It grows near the roots of the Cistus and at its foot, the flowers resembling those of the Pomegranate." The statement that it grows "near" the roots of the Cistus avoids the suggestion that it is parasitic. In general, the early botanists had at best a confused idea of the relation of parasitic plants to their hosts.

All these confusions seem to go back to Dioscorides, who is responsible for calling attention to the alleged resemblance between the flowers of the Hypocistus and those of the Pomegranate—by which he must mean the flowers on the Broomrape which grows on the Pomegranate. Mattioli then adds complications of his own. Apothecaries, he says, should search out the Hypocistus in order to familiarize themselves with it and avoid the common mistake of taking something else to be this important medicinal plant. Usually these apothecaries employ the root of the Goatsbeard where Hypocistus is called for, but if they cannot obtain the latter they should use the juice of wild Pomegranate flowers which, according to Dioscorides, have the same virtues.

HYPOCISTUS

Orobanchaceae : Orobanche

Gooseberry

THE SPINY SHRUB *which Mattioli calls Uva Spina (Prickly grape) is obviously Gooseberry and probably* Ribes grossularia, *English Gooseberry. He seems to think of it as an odd sort of grape for he calls special attention to the fact that the fruit does not come in bunches. Though he is here far off the track (the Gooseberry is actually a Currant), he seems to be correct in saying that the ancients do not appear to have known it. At least nothing which can be identified as a Gooseberry appears in Dioscorides. And that is rather odd since the plant is said to grow wild in parts of Europe, Southwestern Asia, and Africa. Perhaps the Greeks did not like its acrid flavor, but even so that very flavor might have suggested medical uses such as those it acquired in England and, to a lesser extent, in renaissance Italy.*

"The fruits", writes Mattioli, "are full of a juice which is harsh, sour, and astringent and very much like verjuice [i.e. a liquid made from Crab Apples, unripe Grapes, etc. and formerly much used in the kitchen as well as in medicine]. The seeds are tender and are eaten along with the pulp. They are picked in May and June before they are ripe because when ripe they are not agreeable. They are of a cold nature, dry and astringent . . . They are cooked into a sort of porridge for those afflicted with fever. Pregnant women are very fond of them."

It is said that even today Gooseberries are eaten much more often in England than in the United States, and it is noticeable that the English Herbalists are inclined to give a good deal of attention to them. Culpeper assigns them to the influence of Venus and says that they are "exceedingly good to stay the longing of pregnant women". Gooseberries were also believed to give protection against the plague, though Gerard stresses chiefly their culinary use. "The fruit is much used in divers sauces for meats and used in broth instead of verjuice, which maketh the broth not only pleasant to taste but is of great profit to such as are troubled with a hot, burning ague."

Several different explanations have been given of the origin of the common English name, but the most probable is simply that a compote of the berries was a traditional accompaniment of roast goose, much as, in the United States, a turkey implies Cranberries.

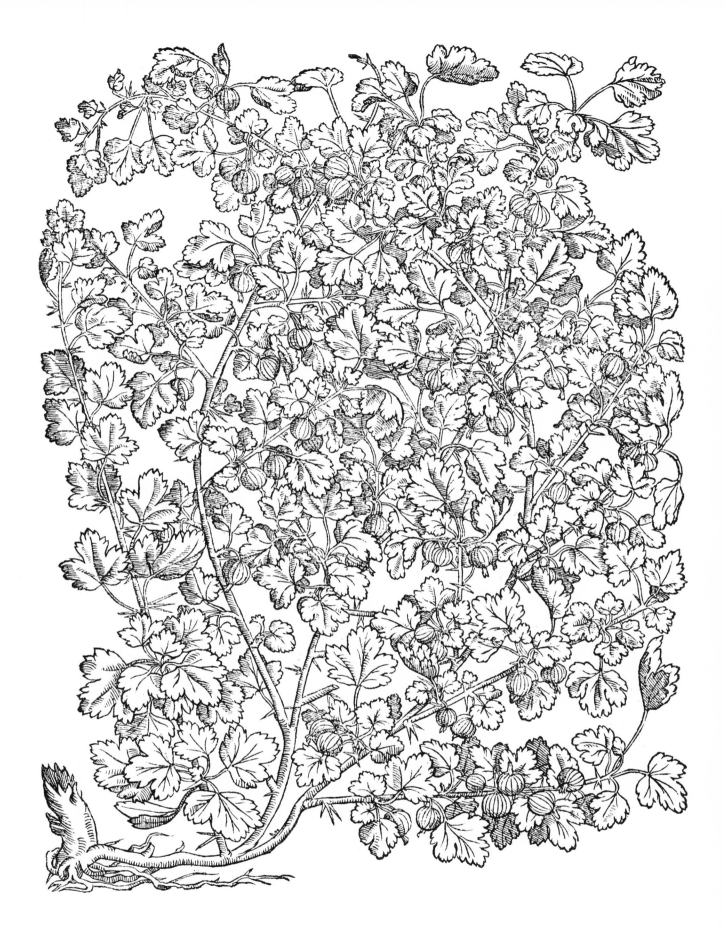

GOOSEBERRY

Saxifragaceae : Ribes

Broomrape

MOST WALKERS *in the woods of either Europe or the United States will recognize this illustration. It represents one of the many species of the* Orobanche *family, all of which send up pallid, faintly purplish shoots about the base of some more substantial plants, and by their ghostly appearance suggest what, in fact, they are—the vampires of the vegetable kingdom.*

"Broomrape" is a common name we have borrowed from England, but different species exploit different plants, though all employ the same technique: They send rootlets into the root of the host and take ready-made nourishment from it. One common New England species (Cancer Root) lives off the Beech tree and one Western species attacks Sagebrush.

Presumably, all the Broomrapes are descended from some self-respecting organism which discovered, perhaps by accident, the trick of living at the expense of a neighbor and gradually lost the green chlorophyll which makes it possible for more normal plants to use the energy of the sun for the manufacture of food.

All of this is, of course, a mere guess, since parasitism in both the animal and plant worlds is one of the great mysteries, and one which seems even greater when we realize that the ancestors of several different parasites must have developed independently along the same lines. Two of the most familiar examples are the Mistletoe, all the species of which are parasitic on trees, and Dodder (actually a member of the otherwise respectable Morning Glory family) which creeps over grain fields. Both differ from the Broomrape in that they send their rootlets into a stem instead of a root.

For some reason, the English Herbalists seem to have been more interested in the Broomrape than those of other countries. Turner describes at some length how it clasps the roots of the Broom, and Culpeper, silly as usual, not only treats Broom and Broomrape as though they were the same, but also drags in his fantastic astrology. "As for Broom and Broomrape, Mars owns them. . . . It is exceedingly prejudicial to the liver, I suppose by reason of the antipathy between Jupiter and Mars."

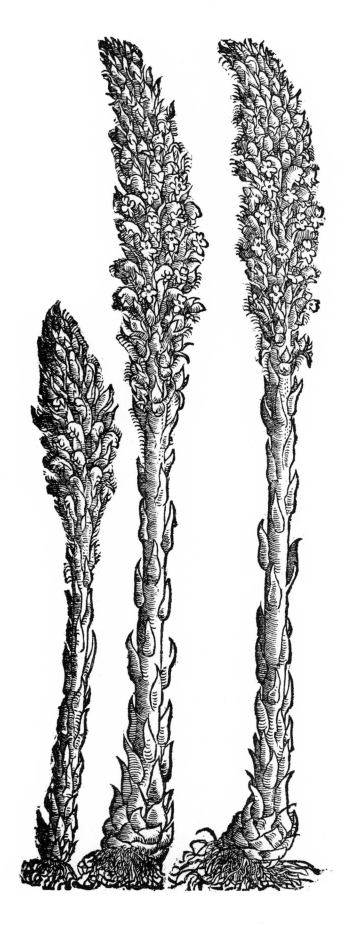

BROOMRAPE

Orobanchaceae : Orobanche

Oats

IN ALL LITERATURE, *the most often cited reference to Oats is certainly the definition in Dr. Johnson's Dictionary: "A grain, which in England, is generally given to horses, but in Scotland supports the people", to which is sometimes added the Scotsman's triumphant rejoinder, "And where else will you find such horses and such men!" Johnson might have found a similarly disparaging opinion of Oats in William Coles'* Adam in Eden, *published more than a century before, where he might have read that "to this day" men as well as beasts eat this grain in some regions such as Wales, Lincolnshire, and Lancashire.*

In the unlikely event that Johnson had read Mattioli he would have found a judgment as severe as his own: "In any case, [Oats] are sown more for animals than for men except in the case of extreme famine when a bread is made of it."

As a matter of fact, all the early writers seem to cherish this prejudice in one form or another. Perhaps it all goes back to a queer notion which Pliny borrows from Theophrastus and which was still accepted by Buffon in the eighteenth century, namely that the Oat is not a separate species but a diseased form of Wheat or Barley and that, as Pliny says, this degeneration, due to weakness of the soil, is so common in Germany that the degenerate seed is sown and Oats used exclusively for porridge.

Gerard, equally unfavorable to Oats as a food, recognizes two kinds, of which the first, Common Oats, is used in many countries to make various kinds of bread, as in Lancashire where it is the most usual grain and is made into cakes; also to make drinks "for want of barley". The second low kind, which he calls Naked Oats, is different from the common in that it can be used as soon as threshed, and without being ground. This provides him with a little joke:

"Some good housewives that delight not to have anything but from hand to mouth . . . go to the barn and rub forth with their hands sufficient for the present time, not willing to provide for the morrow, according as the Scripture speaketh, but let the next day bring forth" [i.e. "Take no thought for the morrow."].

O A T S

Gramineae : Avena

Muskmelon

MODERN BOTANISTS *put the Gourds, Squashes, Pumpkins, and Melons into one big family of about seven hundred species, all of which have separate male and female flowers and nearly all of which are vines which can climb, not by twining, but by means of sensitive tendrils that twist tightly about anything with which they come in contact.*

But when and from where did Europe get this delicious addition to its diet? That is something of a mystery. Our principal species were unknown to the Greeks during the classical age. The Romans confused things by having no separate name for the Melon as distinguished from the Cucumber (botanically a member of the same genus) and that suggests that any Melons they may have had were not very good ones. The first unambiguous reference is in Pliny, where he refers to "Melopepones" which had the color of a Quince and were probably something like our Muskmelons. In the thirteenth century Marco Polo speaks of the best Melons as being found in Chinese Turkestan.

Both Gerard and Parkinson describe Melons as having been grown in England only recently. "[There are] divers sorts of Melons found at this day differing notably in shape and proportion . . . but to the ancients there was only one and no more . . . I have seen at the Queen's house at St. James many . . . ripe through the diligent and curious nourishing of them by a skilful gentleman . . . called Mr. Fowle" (Gerard). Parkinson says that they have only recently been cultivated in England and that the best come from Spain, though some come from France where they were formerly grown only in the gardens of the King or noblemen. They are now more common.

Mattioli devotes a long chapter to Cucumbers and Melons, seeming to recognize only one kind. He struggles long with the classical names and references only to conclude, "As for what the ancients call Melopepones and Pepones, I do not dare say positively that they are what we call Melons and Pompons". On the other hand, his description of the Melons grown in his day makes it seem certain that they were at least something like our Muskmelons.

A modern wit has said that there is nothing which raises so many false hopes as one good Cantaloupe, and the reason is that Cantaloupes have a tendency to relapse into something like the Cucumber, to which they are all-too-closely related.

MUSKMELON

Cucurbitaceae : Cucumis

Coronopus

"CORONOPUS *is a little herb somewhat long, spreading upon the ground, having leaves indented and is eaten as a pot herb.*" *This is almost all that Dioscorides has to say in one of the shortest chapters of his work, but the illustration in the earliest surviving Ms shows what is obviously a member of the Bean family (probably in the genus* Lotus) *and this fits the description well enough. Why there should have been any great mystery I am unable to guess but, for some reason, later Herbalists were thrown into total confusion.*

"I find", writes Mattioli, "that those who have attempted to enrich and illuminate the science of herbs have labored hard to determine what plant should be identified as Coronopus". After devoting hundreds of words to this labor he concludes, oddly enough, that the real Coronopus is a plant totally unlike Dioscorides' description. The illustration is obviously of a member of the Plantain family, probably that baptized Plantago coronopus *by Linnaeus and sometimes called Buckshorn, or Crowfoot Plantain. Gerard, on the other hand, follows Dioscorides closely and offers a plate that will pass very well as a member of that* Lotus *genus of the Bean family to which his Greek forerunner seems to refer.*

As to the Crowfoot Plantain, it is one of a large family of innocuous weeds of no present day use in either official medicine or gardening. In folk medicine, some species are, however, said to be still widely credited with a number of virtues, especially for the treatment of sores and inflammations, including those resulting from bee stings. Coles offers several bits of curious lore as, for instance, the statement that when a toad has been bitten by a spider he will cure himself by eating Plantain.

CORONOPUS

Plantaginaceae : Plantago

Aloe

MODERN BOTANY *recognizes something like one hundred species of Aloe, all native in the warmer regions of the Old World. Many of the species yield a bitter juice having a strong purgative action and a number are grown as ornamentals—as Mattioli notes that they were in his time: "Today one sees Aloes in many parts of Italy, especially in Rome and Naples, where they are tended in pots and boxes filled with earth, rather for the sake of the plant itself as an adornment for the window than for medicinal use; and these plants have not only the white flowers described by Dioscorides but also those which are reddish or purplish."*

In Dioscorides' day the dried juice was imported and used for a variety of ailments as well as for its laxative qualities but, being no doubt scarce, it was sometimes offered in adulterations which Dioscorides warns against. "They counterfeit it with gum, which is detectable by the taste and the bitterness and the strongness of the smell and by its not falling in pieces even to the smallest crumb when squeezed by the fingers. Some also mix Acacia with it."

Though he recommends it to stop "the flux of blood that come from hemorrhoids", Mattioli dares to differ from Dioscorides to the extent of citing another authority who warns that the drug should be avoided by those who have "inflammations of the fundament". Mixed with honey and rubbed on the navel it will expel worms.

According to the English Herbalist William Coles: "[Aloe] is the basis of most pills, for there are few purgative pills which have it not as one chief ingredient."

The dried juice of several species is still recognized as official by the U.S. Pharmacopoeia, though not regarded with as much favor as it was in the days before the less irritating Cascara became available from the bark of a New World Buckthorn.

ALOE

Liliaceae : Aloe

Meadowsweet

MATTIOLI *calls the plant shown here* Filipendula *and we will give him the benefit of any doubts there may be, especially since he is at great pains to demonstrate that various distinguished authorities before him have confused it with a very different herb mentioned by Dioscorides. (This kind of thing might be, one must realize, very serious, and the physician guilty of it runs the risk of prescribing a hot plant when a cold one is called for, or administering a remedy for the bite of a mad dog to a patient suffering from asthma.)*

In any event, Mattioli's Filipendula *is certainly either that or a* Spiraea *—both of which genera belong to the enormous Rose family, and are familiar garden subjects as well as wild flowers common in both hemispheres. Popular names also are confusing but various species are familiarly called Meadowsweet and Queen of the Meadows.*

The species illustrated may well be what Linnaeus baptized Spiraea ulmaria *and more recent taxonomists have been pleased to change to* Filipendula ulmaria. *It has rather showy white flowers, and though native to Europe and Asia is to some extent naturalized in the United States.*

The distilled liquid of the flowers was said to relieve itching and burning eyes, and in Chaucer's Knights Tale *the knights about to enter into combat apply various magical ointments and drink a concoction called Save, into the composition of which Meadowsweet was said to enter. It did not, however, protect Arcite, whose breast wound was desperate, "so that neither bleeding nor cupping nor herb decoctions could help him". (Incidentally, this whole passage, lines 1840 ff, is a vivid death scene described in terms of medieval medicine.)*

Meadowsweet, however, was especially valued for its fragrance. Gerard calls it both Meadowsweet and Queen of the Meadows and says that in England it grows at the edge of water ditches and riversides, as well as in meadows.

"The leaves and flowers far excel all other strewing herbs, for to deck up houses in the summer time; for the smell thereof makes the heart merry, delighteth the senses; neither doth it cause headache, or loathsomeness to meat, as some other sweet smelling herbs do."

MEADOWSWEET

Rosaceae: Filipendula

Cedar of Lebanon

ONE OF THE *minor but frequent pleasures of the botanist consists in correcting laymen who say "Cedar" when they should be saying "Juniper". One way to distinguish between them is by knowing that the fruit of the Juniper is berry-like while that of the Cedar is a cone. It appears that even the Old Testament sometimes confuses the two, and Mattioli was much distressed to find that Dioscorides was seemingly guilty of the same error. Later he was gratified to learn that this seeming error was the result of a corruption of the text. Nowadays we rather like to demonstrate how wrong our predecessors were, but during the Renaissance men did not like to admit that their revered authorities were fallible.*

The most famous of all Cedars is, of course, the Cedar of Lebanon (Cedrus libani). *It is a handsome tree which grows to a height of eighty feet or more and is often cultivated in the United States and in Europe. But its chief fame is literary, or one might almost say, religious, since it appears time and again in the Old Testament, where it is called "excellent above all trees of the field" and figures as a symbol of power, prosperity, and long life. If the eighty thousand wood cutters said to have been employed by Solomon really did confine themselves exclusively to Lebanon Cedars, it is a wonder that any trees survived. Actually, though the most famous grove—that about fifteen miles from Beirut—is much reduced and perhaps dying out there are said to be considerable forests elsewhere.*

One of the first Europeans ever to see a Lebanon Cedar was probably the Frenchman Pierre Belon, who was moved by scientific curiosity rather than piety when he visited the Near East in 1550 to gather material for his De Arboris Coniferis, *said to be the first book ever written on the cone-bearing trees. He reports that the grove was under the control of the Patriarch of the Maronite Christians of Beirut, and that this priest first celebrated a high mass under the trees and then issued a solemn warning against harming them in any way. The first specimen ever seen in England was brought in 1641 by Edward Pococke, who had been a chaplain at Aleppo. Nearly a century later, Bernard de Jussieu, the great proposer of the so-called "natural" system of classification, got from England the first specimen set out in the Jardin des Plantes in Paris. Now the Cedar of Lebanon is common in cultivation.*

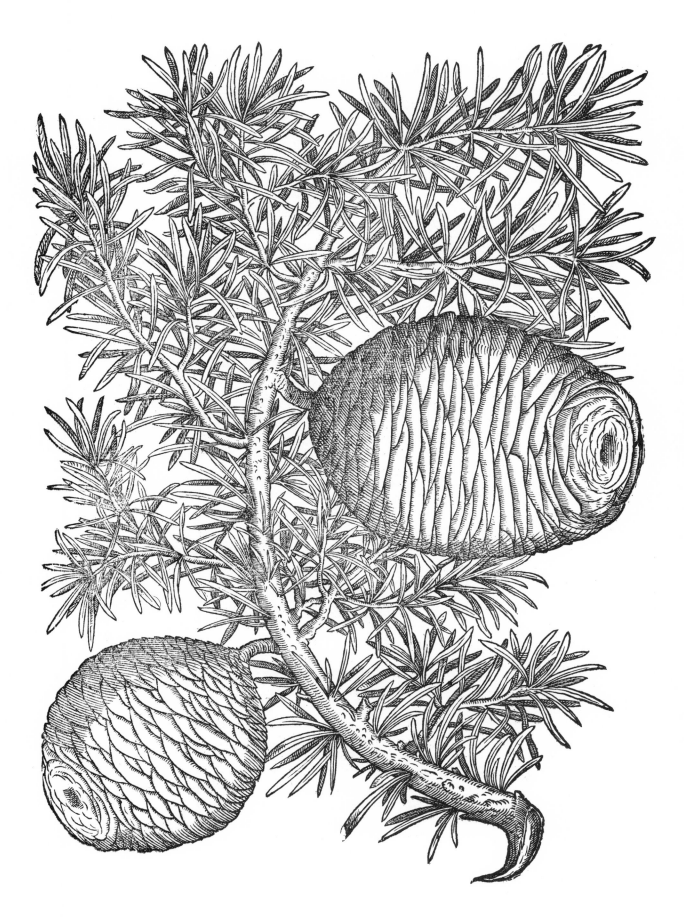

CEDAR OF LEBANON

Pinaceae : Cedrus

Cherry

ALMOST ALL *of our familiar temperate-climate fruits—Apple, Pear, Quince, Plum, and Cherry—were known to Dioscorides, though he treats most of them so briefly that it is usually difficult to say how close to the modern types his varieties are. All belong to the same great Rose family; all are closely related one to another; and all have wild cousins scattered widely over the temperate parts of the globe. Yet, one of our commonest fruits the ancients apparently did not have: the Peach. It seems to have been introduced from Asia Minor in post-classical times.*

Of the Cherry, Pliny says that there are nine varieties but that they were not grown in Italy "before the period of the victory of the city gained over Mithridates by Lucullus in the year 680. He was the first to introduce the tree from Pontus and now, in the course of one hundred and twenty years, it has travelled beyond the oceans and arrived even in Briton".

Mattioli illustrates three varieties and describes several others, including the bitter Maraschino (which should be, but usually isn't, the kind so frequently met with at cocktail parties). He is struck by the exuberant flourishing of this introduced tree:

"Some are bitter, some harsh, some sour, and some tasteless . . . The soil of Italy was so suited to them that not only those deliberately planted but also those not in any way cultivated soon spread over mountain and plain, valley and forest." Then he adds a strange and dubious bit of lore: All kinds of cherries lose their character if they are manured in any way, so great is their hatred of every kind of dung. On the other hand, they flourish if branches cut from the tree are buried about its base.

Apparently, the Cherry took readily to the English soil and climate also. Parkinson in the early seventeenth century speaks of there being so many varieties "that I know not well how to express them . . . For eating the sweet are most pleasant, the sour more wholesome. In France, sour cherries are dried like prunes and given to the sick in all hot fevers. The gum of the tree is said to be good for gravel or stone".

CHERRY

Rosaceae : Prunus

Scabiosa

GARDENERS *are sometimes vaguely, and perhaps subconsciously, disturbed by the fact that the name of so easily grown a flower should carry an unpleasant suggestion. But the sound is no coincidence. Here is one of the cases where both the botanical and the common name of a plant derive from its "signature". As Coles says, it is called Scabiosa "quod scabei meditur which it doeth by signature . . . It brings forth cups which stand on the tops of the stalks like unto scale or scabs". The only other genus of the family which has ornamental or utilitarian significance is the Teasel, sometimes grown for its attractiveness (as in dried bouquets) or for its use in "teasing" woolen cloth.*

Gerard speaks of two kinds which grow almost everywhere in pastures, meadows, cornfields and barren sandy grounds. Two of the European species are now established in the northeastern part of the American continent. "The strange sorts", Gerard goes on, "grow in my garden, yet are they strangers in England". Of the English wild species, Parkinson (a gardener rather than an Herbalist) says that since they have no flowers of beauty he will leave them in the fields where they live.

In addition to curing skin disorders, the Scabiosa was thought by Mattioli to be effective against chest troubles and especially valuable as a sudorific, very effective against the plague in its early stage. Gerard says that according to "the later Herbalists" it is good for snake bite. Since an astonishingly long list of herbs was thought to serve this purpose, one can only conclude that few ever died from the bite of the mostly non-poisonous European snakes.

Scabiosus is either not mentioned by Dioscorides (which is odd since it is native to southern Europe) or is described in such a way as to preclude identification. Yet it must have been well known in the Middle Ages since it figures in the recipe for a medicinal bath given in the fifteenth-century manuscript of John Russell's Book of Nature. *The author was Usher and Marshal to Humphrey, Duke of Gloucester, and his duties included bathing his master. Among the twenty herbs to go into the bath, Scabiosa figures as a cure for (or preventative of) the itch. Marshmallow, Fennel, and Henbane are also included, and the water in which all these herbs have been steeped is to be made "as hot as he may abide".*

SCABIOSA

Dipsacaceae : Scabiosa

Water Chestnut

THE WATER CHESTNUT *itself is a huge, four-horned, one-seeded fruit, shiny black and so outlandish in appearance as to provoke a "What-on-earth-is-that" from those who have never seen it before. In the Middle Ages, pilgrims anxious to impress the natives with their large-scale piety wore strings of Water Chestnuts around their necks as oversized rosaries.*

The freakish looking seed was called Tribolos *by the Greeks,* Tribulus *by the Latins, and* Caltrops *by the Herbalists—the last name being derived from a fancied resemblance to the spiked iron balls strewn on the ground to impede the advance of an enemy cavalry. It comes from a rather handsome aquatic which is native to Southern Europe and Asia and is sometimes grown in water gardens here.*

Dioscorides says that the Thracians who live by the River Strymon fatten horses with the green plant, but keep the sweet, wholesome nuts for themselves. According to Mattioli it grows in various parts of Italy, especially in the regions of Farrara and Mantua, but also in salt water at Venice. He adds that it has the taste of the chestnut and that "the common people" eat it in the same way or, in time of famine, make a kind of bread out of it.

As for its medical uses, Dioscorides says that Tribolos is cooling and binding when taken internally and as a cataplasm good for all inflammations. Mixed with honey, it heals inflamed tonsils and ulcers of the mouth and gums. Sprinkled about the house it kills fleas.

Nature has played one little trick which seems intended to lead the Herbalists astray. She created and made native to the same region as the Water Chestnut a prostrate land plant which bears spine-pointed seeds half the size of a pea, and in form much like miniature Water Chestnuts. Inevitably the two plants were assumed to be closely related; were called respectively Tribolos terrestris *and* Tribolos aquatious; *and assigned the same medicinal virtues. Actually, however, they resemble one another in no other respect and belong in quite different families. Linnaeus straightened the matter out by renaming the water plant* Trapa natans *and keeping* Tribolos terrestris *for the other.*

Note that the Water Chestnut discussed here is not the sliced root which is also so called and figures prominently in Chinese dishes.

WATER CHESTNUT

Onagraceae: Trapa

Beaver

188 TO ANCIENT *and medieval medicine, the Beaver contributed a musk-like substance, until recently (and perhaps still) used in certain perfumes. It is produced in special glands which the old writers wrongly believed to be the testicles, and that belief led to a persistent legend.*

Dioscorides protested the "vain report" that when Beavers are pursued by hunters they attempt to save their lives by biting off their testicles and leaving them behind. More than a thousand years later the Bestiaries not only continue to tell the story, but deduce from it an excellent moral:

"Hence every man who inclines toward the commandment of God and who wants to live chastely, must cut off from himself all vices, all notions of lewdness and must cast them from him in the Devil's face. Thereupon the Devil, seeing him to have nothing of his own about him, goes away from him confused."

Mattioli explicitly rejects the authority of various ancients who report the Beaver's self-castration, and Sir Thomas Browne, in one of his fascinating if not quite English sentences, remarks: "The original of the conceit was probably Hieroglyphical [symbolical], which later became Mythological unto the Greeks and is so set down by Aesop, and by process of tradition stole into total verity."

BEAVER

Oak

OF THE *two or three hundred species of Oak recognized in modern botany, Dioscorides treats only three, and treats them quite briefly at that. Nevertheless, no other tree (not even the Laurel) has ever had what one is tempted to call a better press, in either prose or verse. Oaks are always "sturdy" and always ready to lend support to clinging vines. Everyone knows that they were worshiped by the Druids and that the English have had a tendency to assume a sort of proprietary interest in a tree whose many virtues are, they like to suppose, parallel to their own. But celebrations of the Oak go much further back. Thus Pliny, after describing its utility, calls attention also to the fact that it symbolizes the highest honor:*

"It is with the leaves of this class of trees that our civic crown is made, the most glorious reward that can be bestowed on military valor, and for this long time past the emblem of the Imperial clemency. Far inferior to this are the mural crown, the valor, and the golden one, superior though they may be in the value of the material."

Culpeper calls the Oak "so well known (the timber thereof being the glory and safety of the British nation) that it needeth no description"; Kipling, perhaps the last heart-of-oak English poet, sings:

> *Of all the trees that grow so fair,*
> *Old England to adorn,*
> *Greater are none beneath the sun,*
> *Than Oak, and Ash, and Thorn!*

Even the United States Army has its Oak Leaf Clusters, bestowed as an additional honor on those already decorated for exceptional service.

Few, if any, other groups of plants are discussed at greater length by Mattioli, who begins thus with the chief uses in medicine:

"All the trees that bear acorns are astringent, especially that rind which is between the bark and the wood . . . A decoction is good for those who spit blood and against colics, dysenteries, and discharges from the stomach . . . Mashed and made into a suppository the immoderate flux of women is arrested. The Acorn has the same virtues . . . A decoction of the Acorn, its bark and its skin, drunk with cow's milk is used against the bites and stings of venomous creatures."

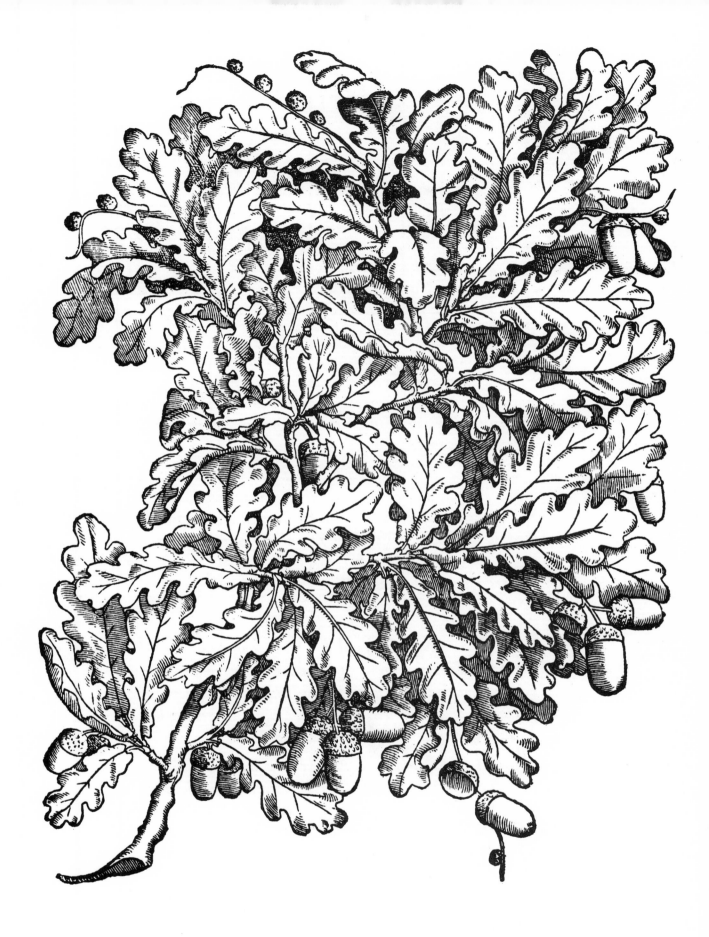

O A K

Fagaceae : Quercus

Carrot

MOST OF *the important food plants and most of the domestic animals have been so changed by millenia of artificial selection that it is impossible to say positively what wild species they descend from. The Carrot, on the other hand, is a striking exception. Taxonomists can find no characteristic fundamental enough to justify their calling it specifically distinct from the common weed* Daucus carrota, *sometimes called Wild Carrot but more familiar to Americans as Queen Anne's Lace. Europe is its homeland, but it has long been established and abundant in parts of the United States.*

Since it is a biennial and therefore requires a second year to flower, we seldom see a mature garden Carrot because we dig it up at the end of its first season, for the sake of the thick root formed in preparation for next year's flowering. The size of this root is the only difference between the wild Carrot and the tame.

Daucus *was an ancient Greek name and the first known appearance of the word Carrot is in the work of Athenaeus, the garrulous scholar who flourished in the second century* A.D. *The ancients seemed to have confused the Carrot with the Parsnip (a quite distinct genus and species of the same family). This problem of classification was not settled until the magisterial Linnaeus took the matter in hand and refused to recognize the cultivated Carrot as specifically distinct, while putting the Parsnip in a genus of its own.*

Mattioli, however, recognizes the close kinship of Daucus *with Corriander and Cumin (all members of the same family) and follows Dioscorides in saying that the seeds of all three stimulate urination, provoke the menstrual flow, and hasten childbirth. Drunk with wine they sooth spider bites; applied as a plaster they heal tumors.*

The English Herbalists inherited all the confusions concerning the distinctions to be made or not made between wild Carrots and tame, and between Carrot and Parsnip. Turner is distressed that some otherwise-instructed Herbalists make serious mistakes in this matter and Culpeper offers a generalization: "The garden sorts are of less physical use than the wild kind (as indeed almost in all herbs the wild are the most effective in physics, as being more powerful in their operations than the garden kinds)."

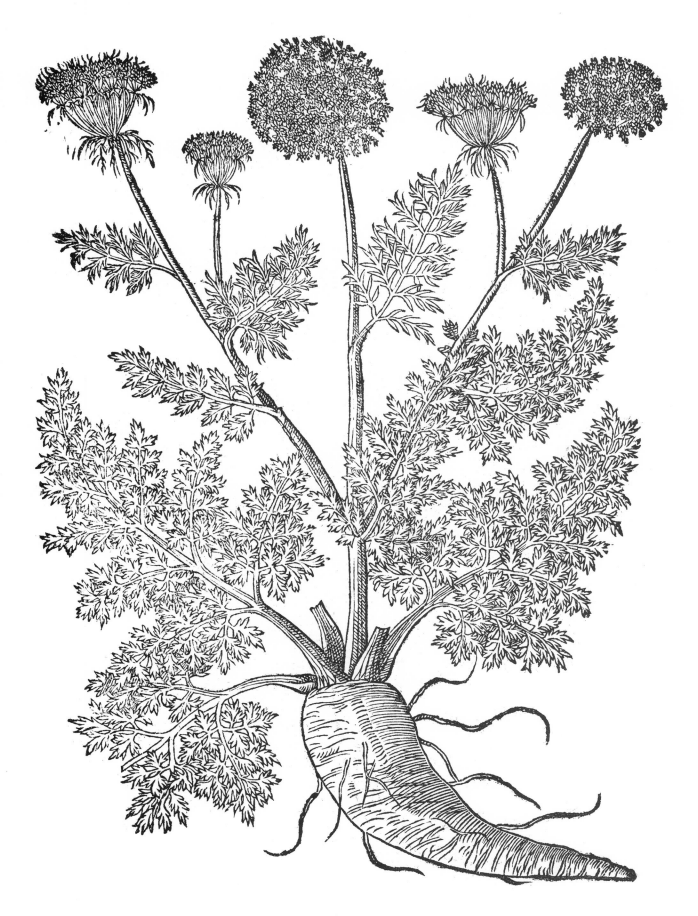

CARROT

Umbelliferae : Daucus

Butcher's Broom

BUTCHER'S BROOM (Ruscus aculeatus) *is a low-growing, stiff, and prickly evergreen shrub with spine-tipped leaves. Since the male and female flowers are borne on different plants it is, like the Mulberry, the Date, and quite a number of other species, what the botanists call dioecious. But the Herbalists, not understanding sexuality in the vegetable kingdom, failed to recognize its true nature, though they often called two distinct species of the same genus the male and female forms of the same species simply because one was larger or coarser than the other.*

Butcher's Broom is a member of the Lily family and therefore not at all related to the other familiar Brooms, either wild or cultivated. It owes its name to the fact that in Italy, at least, butchers were accustomed to use it to clean their chopping blocks. It is also sometimes called Jew's Myrtle because of its use during the Feast of the Tabernacles. The young shoots were eaten like Asparagus—which is not as surprising as it might at first sight seem, since Asparagus also is a member of the Lily family. Though a native of southern Europe, Butcher's Broom is widely grown in England and sometimes in the warmer parts of the United States— less for the sake of its inconspicuous flowers or its red or yellow berries than as part of a dry winter bouquet. It is often dyed red, especially at Christmas time.

Dioscorides dismisses Ruscus *in a few lines, and of its virtues says only: "The hair seems to be an amulet profitable for the headaches. And the root and juice are mixed also with malagma." Parkinson says it is used not only as a butcher's broom but also "to protect 'hanged meat' from mice". From the later Herbals it would seem that its reputation as a medicine tended to grow. Culpeper recommends it either as a poultice or drunk in a decoction to knit broken bones. It was also highly regarded as a remedy for dropsy and as a diuretic because, as Mattioli says, "it cures those who cannot urinate except drop by drop".*

BUTCHER'S BROOM

Liliaceae : Ruscus

Radish

FROM ANCIENT DAYS *on the Radish seems to have got a rather bad press, perhaps in part for the reason which has made it a favorite with beginning gardeners—namely, that it is abundant and will all but grow itself. The Radish, says Dioscorides, "breeds winds and heats, is welcome to the mouth but not good for the stomach, besides it causeth belching and is uretical".*

For some reason, Pliny treats it at great length and offers his usual entertaining farrago. The Greeks, he says, are such a frivolous people that (so it is said) they give special honor to the Radish in the temple of Apollo at Delphi by representing it in gold, the Beet in silver, the Rape in lead. There is so great an antipathy between it and the Grape Vine that the latter will shrink away from a Radish if planted near it.

Some millennium and a half later Culpeper is warning, "Sleep not presently after eating of the Radish; that will cause a stinking breath". King Lear calls man a mere forked Radish because, of all the plants which have forked roots, the Radish is of least account. "Radishes", says Pliny, "are flatulent to a remarkable degree and are productive of eructations; hence it is that they are looked upon as an aliment only fit for low people, and this more particularly if Coleworts are eaten directly after them. If on the other hand they are eaten with green Olives, the eructations are not so frequent and less offensive."

His account of the life history of a certain butterfly is interesting because in every respect except one it represents a quite accurate observation. When dew on a Radish leaf has been "thickened by the sun" it becomes reduced to the size of a millet [actually, of course, this is an egg]. From this, a small grub emerges and soon becomes a caterpillar. Then, for several successive days it still increases in size but remains motionless and becomes covered with a hard husk. It moves only when touched and is covered with a web like a spider. In this state it is called a chrysalis, but after the husk is broken it flies forth in the shape of a butterfly.

Cuvier remarks that this is a very correct account of the life history of the common Cabbage Butterfly, which lays its eggs on various members of the Mustard family—except, of course, that the Romans and Greeks did not recognize the eggs of a creature they assumed to be "generated by corruption".

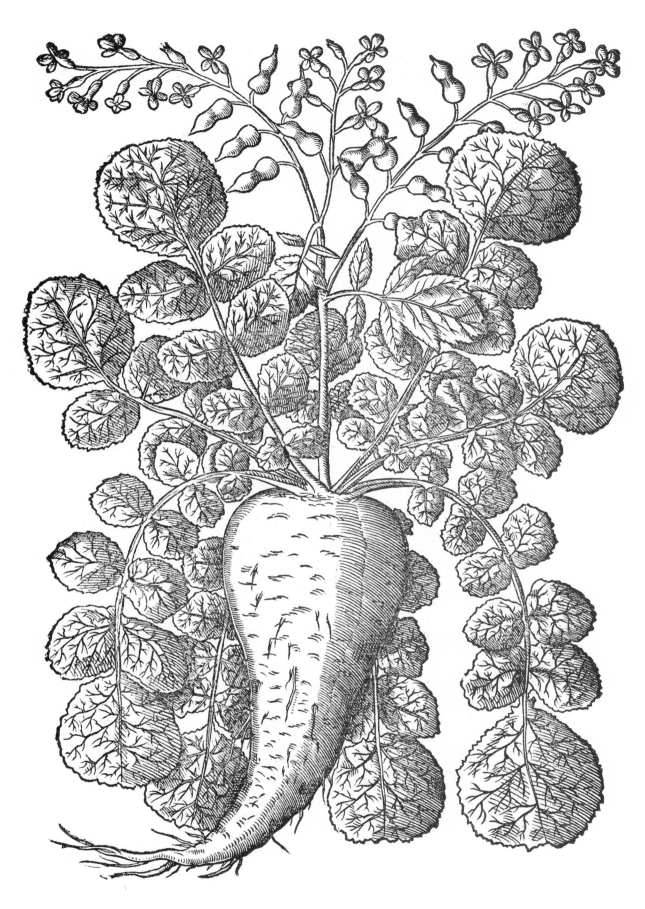

RADISH

Cruciferae : Raphanus

Mountain Ash

THERE ARE *eighty or more species of this attractive tree including our own* S. americana, *common in the East, and the* S. sitchensis *of the West. Rowan, Service Tree, and Mountain Ash are common English names, though the last is misleading since* Sorbus *is actually a member of the Rose family and resembles an Ash in nothing save the shape of its leaves.*

Dioscorides says only that if the yellow (unripe) berries are dried in the sun then they are "binding", either eaten as a porridge or drunk as a concoction. Mattioli adds nothing concerning medicinal virtues but tells us that the ripe red berries have a pleasant odor and taste; that the wood, being extremely tough, is in great demand for making tables; and that ox-drivers use it for their goads.

The Druids are said to have planted Sorbus *near their stone circles as a protection against evil spirits. Probably they took it to be one of the true Ashes (to which it is not related) and, therefore, a sharer in the magical potency which was so widely attributed to the latter. In Scandinavian mythology, Yggdrasil, the World Tree, was an Ash and down to the present day many superstitions are connected with it. Pliny tells us that he knows from his own experience that if a snake be confined within a circle composed in part of fire and in part of branches of the Ash, it will escape across the fire rather than touch the Ash. "It is", he goes on, "a wonderful courtesy of nature that the Ash should flower before the serpents appear and not cast its leaves before they are gone again" (i.e. into hibernation).*

In England, children were passed through a cleft in an Ash to cure them of rupture or rickets, and it is said that there is a "Shrew Tree" still standing in Richmond Park which owes its name to a magical rite described by Gilbert White as recently practiced in his eighteenth-century village. Lameness in cattle or horses was caused by a Shrew which had crept over one of their limbs. It could be cured by gently rubbing the afflicted limb with the branches of an Ash which had been made potent by a live Shrew left to die in a plugged hole in the tree. Says White: "Near the church there stood about twenty years ago . . . a Shrew Ash . . . As the ceremonies necessary for such a consecration are no longer known, all succession is at an end and no such tree is known to exist in the manor."

MOUNTAIN ASH

Rosaceae : Sorbus

Spurge

SPURGE *is a popular name for various herbs in the enormous* Euphorbia *family. There are something like four thousand species, some of them tree-like. They are distributed around the world and very many have a thick, milky juice which is violently purgative and poisonous. Para rubber comes from a member of the family, and so does the Mexican Jumping Bean.*

During the Middle Ages, Spurge was one of the best known medicinal herbs, and in Chaucer the practical minded wife of Chanticleer recommended it to dispel his bad dreams by "purging you below and also above". Nevertheless, the Herbalists were cautious about recommending it. Thus Gerard writes:

"These herbs, by my advice, should not be received into the body, considering that there be so many other good and wholesome potions to be made with other herbs." He can, he goes on, speak from experience, since when he took into his mouth but one drop of a Spurge growing by the sea . . . "[it] nevertheless did so influence and swell my throat that I hardly escaped with my life". Many of the Euphorbias do, in fact, have a juice which will blister the skin. If even the smoke of the burning wood gets into one's eyes it can cause serious trouble, and this is the source of the belief that certain Mexican trees will cause blindness in anyone who incautiously sleeps in their shelter.

Mattioli describes and pictures the related Castor Bean also. It is the source of castor oil and the only member of the family still used to any extent in medicine. This ornamental, rankly growing plant originated somewhere in the tropics but has been established in the warmer parts of the world since very early times. It was familiar enough in Europe to be mentioned by Herodotus as though already well known in classical Greece. It owes the first part of its botanical name, Ricinus communis, *to the supposed resemblance of its curiously marked seeds to the dog tick which is called* Ricinus *in Latin. These seeds are deadly poison, and the oil must be treated to remove certain alkaloids before it is used as a purgative.*

A common name for the Castor Bean was Christ's Thorn; and according to one specialist on the plants of the Bible, it was probably the tree under which Noah rested.

SPURGE

Euphorbiaceae : Euphorbia

Oak Gall

THE OAKS *are exceptionally subject to those vegetable tumors called "galls", which are provoked by a great variety of insects whose eggs and larvae are protected by the morbid growths. By now, more than three hundred different kinds have been named on the Oak alone, but the early botanists were not quite sure what to make of them and, in at least one instance (that of the so-called Kermes Oak, see page 208), they definitely mistook a gall for the fruit of the tree.*

Even when they knew that an insect was often associated with the gall they did not clearly understand that the creature was responsible for its existence. Dioscorides explicitly calls certain galls "the fruit of the oak" and discusses their medicinal uses. Mattioli also calls special attention to them and, a good many years later, Gerard gives an interesting account in which observation and superstition are thoroughly mixed. Of what he calls the Oak Apple (obviously very similar, at least, to the hollow balls common on American Oaks and made by a tiny relative of the Ichneuman flies) he says that Kentish husbandmen have observed that the insect found in a gall announces the favorableness or unfavorableness of the coming season. "If they find an Ant they foretell plenty of grain to ensue; if a white worm like a Gentil or a maggot then they prognosticate murrain of beasts and cattle; if a spider then (they say) we shall have pestilence or some such sickness to follow among men. These things the learned also have observed and noted, for Mattioli saith that before they have an hole through them, they contain in them either a fly, a spider, or a worm; if a fly then war ensueth, if a creeping worm, then scarcity of victuals, if a running spider, then followeth great sickness and mortality."

Certain galls survive in modern medicine at least to the extent that there is a U.S.P. fluid extract of one. Ink was made from a Chinese kind, and the Allepo Galls made by a wasp are said to be what appear in literature as the Dead Sea, or Sodom, Apples.

OAK GALL

Fagaceae : Quercus

Onion

MODERN BOTANY *puts Onions, Leeks, and Garlic all in the genus Allium. The ancients were familiar with all three, recognized the kinship between them (who could miss it?), and described several kinds of each.*

Despite the various medicinal virtues claimed and still claimed (at least in folk medicine), there seems to have been always something ambiguous in the attitude toward them as food.

In Greek and Latin as well as in modern literature, the stinking breath of the polloi is a commonplace, and of Chaucer's Pardoner, the most unpleasant character among his pilgrims, it is said that he "well loved the garlic, onions, aye and leeks".

Very ancient associations with magic no doubt suggested the sacred-accursed ambiguity of the taboo. According to Pliny, Garlic and Onions were invoked by the Egyptians in taking an oath, and according to other ancient authorities the inhabitants of Pelusium (an ancient Egyptian city) were devoted to the worship of the Onion and held Garlic in great aversion as a food. A variety of superstitions concerning Onions and Garlic is widespread, and many are found in modern as well as in ancient times. The juice of roasted Onion will cure earache; a raw Onion placed under the pillow on St. Thomas' Eve will bring dreams of one's future spouse. Settlers of New England brought with them strings of Onions to hang over doorways as a protection against infections. A twelfth-century Jewish physician recommends Onion juice rubbed on the penis as a contraceptive. Roman soldiers ate Garlic in the belief that it gave them courage; and Bolivian Indians believe that a bull will not charge anyone carrying Garlic. Pliny mentions the belief that a magnet loses its power if rubbed with Garlic, and sixteen hundred years later Sir Thomas Browne still finds this Vulgar Error current.

A fading taboo often becomes comic and Garlic and Onion were already comic in Shakespeare's time. When Enobarbus wants to suggest that Anthony is not sorrowing for his wife, he says, "The tears live in an onion that should water this sorrow", thus playing with a very old joke vide *the advice, "get an Onion", given in the thriteenth-century Romance of the Rose to a lover who can't produce enough tears to arouse the pity of a reluctant mistress.*

O N I O N

Liliaceae: Allium

Bee

IN THE ANCIENT WORLD *and throughout the Middle Ages everyone knew that Bees were generated out of the decaying bodies of oxen, and that the hive was ruled over by a king, not a queen. As to the first of these facts, compare Sampson's riddle ("Out of the strong came forth sweetness"). As to the second, see Shakespeare's* Henry V, *where the queen is called an emperor; or, more picturesquely, see the Bestiary where we may read: "They arrange their own king for themselves . . . The king does not merely hold the privilege of judgment, but he also excites a feeling of allegiance both because the Bees love him on the ground that he was appointed by themselves and also because they honor him for being at the head of so great a swarm."*

Until the establishment of commerce with the New World, honey was, of course, the most available sweetening, while cane sugar was rare, expensive, and considered as either a medicine or a very exotic confection. That it was, however, not unknown to the Greeks is indicated by the few lines Dioscorides devotes to what he calls Sakcharon: "There is a kind of concreted Honey called sugar, found in reeds in India and Arabia Felix, like in consistency to salt, and brittle to be broken between the teeth, as salt is. It is good for the belly and stomach, being dissolved in water and so drank; helping the pained bladder and the reines."

BEE

Kermes Oak

IT IS USUALLY *easy enough to answer correctly the traditional question "animal, vegetable, or mineral?". But not always. And one of the most persistent of the wrong answers was that given for centuries to the so-called Kermes Oak* (Quercus coccifera), *a shrub oak which bears, in addition to acorns, certain bodies long known as Kermes "berries".*

The name Kermes is Arabic for crimson. The "berries" supplied a dye which is mentioned by Moses and is probably one of the earliest used by man. Early in the sixteenth century, however, the Spaniards brought back from Mexico a superior dye of the same sort, furnished by a dried insect called Cochineal, which infests a certain species of Prickly Pear Cactus.

It was almost two hundred years after the Cochineal had displaced it as a commercially important product that the true nature of the Kermes "berry" was recognized. It is actually a gall, being the swollen body of a scale insect closely related to the Cochineal. Some members of this family are destructive pests, others are the source of a lacquer, used since prehistoric times by American Indians as well as by the orientals, and all have very odd life histories.

At one stage, the Kermes insects are tiny but very active creatures which swarm over the host plant; later attach themselves to fissures in its bark, to buds or, occasionally, to leaves. Some months thereafter they become greatly distended with a red juice and again quite inactive until, presently, numerous eggs are extruded. It was during this quiet period that they were collected, dried and, if intended for medical use, mixed into a paste.

The ancients used the paste diluted with vinegar for wounds, and during the Middle Ages the dye was an ingredient in a widely used medicine called Confection alkermes, *which remained long an official astringent in the London Pharmacopoeia.*

All such preparations have by now been discarded by medical practitioners, and the Cochineal which superseded Kermes as a dye has, in its turn, been largely superseded by synthetic dyes for most purposes, including that of harmlessly coloring foods and confections. For this last it was widely used well into our own century.

KERMES OAK

Fagaceae : Quercus

Narcissus

TO THE GREEKS, *"Narcissus" suggested either a beautiful boy or a beautiful flower, but in our unromantic day it is more likely to suggest a neurotic. All three are, of course, connected, but one may begin with the flower. Modern botany has adopted the Greek word as the technical name for a genus of the Amaryllis family, which includes some twenty-five or thirty original species now split into innumerable horticultural varieties. Among them are the flowers we call Daffodil and Jonquil as well as those we call Narcissus.*

But what did the Greeks mean when they used the word? They didn't mean what we call "Daffodil", for that is merely a corruption of "As-phodel", and the Greeks gave that name to a quite different flower. On the other hand, Dioscorides' description seems quite clear: "Narcissus is like in the leaves to the Leek, but they are thinner and smaller by much and narrower. It has a stalk which is empty, without leaves, longer than a span; on which is a white flower, but within of a saffron color." This can hardly be anything except our commonest Narcissus (N. poeticus).

According to Dioscorides, the Narcissus is (most unpoetically) a good emetic if you eat the root. Being beaten, mixed with honey, and laid on the skin it helps "long continued griefs about the joints"—which modern physicians seem to have forgotten.

As for the legend which every schoolboy once knew: Narcissus would have none of the nymphs who loved him and especially he would not have Echo, who must, indeed, have been rather tiresome because, having been cursed by Juno, she could only repeat what others said to her. His obduracy completed one of those A-loves-B who-loves-C circles so useful to comedy writers, and inspired the poet Moscus with a moral:

> *Thus all, while their true lovers' hearts they grieved,*
> *Were scorned in turn, and what they gave received.*
> *O, all love's scorners, learn this lesson true:*
> *Be kind to love, that he be kind to you.*

One day, Narcissus happened to see his own image reflected in the water, fell in love for the first time, and pined away with longing until he died. Moreover, he was so far from cured of his infatuation that, while being transported in Charon's boat, he leaned over the edge to get one last look at himself as reflected in the waters of the Styx.

210

NARCISSUS

Amaryllidaceae : Narcissus

Dandelion

THE DANDELION *is not a native of the United States but it has made itself thoroughly at home here, as in many of the other temperate regions of the globe. Its numerous, efficiently windborn seeds; its perennial, almost indestructible root; and its undemanding nature so far as soil, moisture, etc. are concerned have made it eminently "fit to survive", and even to inherit the earth. Every man's hand is against it and we call it "weed", not "wild flower", just because it is so common and so commonly where we do not want it to be. Its beauty may be plebeian but it is very real, though Walt Whitman is the only major poet ever to celebrate it:*

> *Simple and fresh and fair at winter's close emerging,*
> *As if no artifice of fashion, business, politics, had ever been,*
> *Forth from its sunny nook of shelter'd grass—innocent,*
> > *golden, calm as the dawn,*
> *The spring's first dandelion shows its trustful face.*

Botanically, the Dandelion belongs with the Chicories and Endives in that section of the Composite *family whose members exude a bitter, milky juice. Rather surprisingly it is unrecorded by Dioscorides and is said to be first mentioned as a medicine by an Arabian physician of the tenth century* A.D.

After reminding us that the Dandelion is "vulgarly called Piss-a-bed", Culpeper proceeds enthusiastically thus:

"The root going downwards exceedingly deep, which being broken off within the ground will notwithstanding shoot forth again and will hardly be destroyed when it hath once taken deep root in the ground. It is under the dominion of Venus . . . and very effectual for the obstructions of the liver, gall and spleen . . . You see here what virtues this common herb hath and that is the reason the French and Dutch so often eat them in the spring."

The usual assumption that Dandelion is a corruption of dent-de-lion *and that it refers to the shape of the leaf is sometimes questioned. But it is the explanation already given in the fifteenth-century* Hortus Sanitatis *and by implication in Turner's Herbal, where it is called Dan-de-Lyon.*

In addition to its use as a salad, the Dandelion makes a country wine and the roasted root is sometimes used, like Chicory, as a coffee substitute.

DANDELION

Compositae : Taraxacum

Pomegranate

IN THE UNITED STATES, *the Pomegranate is no more than a novelty fruit, and in the warmer regions is more likely to be grown as an ornamental than for its edible but not very substantial fruit. Nevertheless, it has been in cultivation since prehistoric times and was formerly far more esteemed. "I would cause thee to drink of the spiced wine of my Pomegranate", promises* The Song of Solomon.

The modern botanical name is from the classical Latin Malum punicum, *or Carthage Apple, because the tree was supposed to have been introduced from North Africa. Dioscorides speaks of what he calls, curiously, "Pomegranate Flowers"—by which he means those of a Broomrape parasitic on the Pomegranate tree. (Compare with Hypocistus, page 164.)*

The Pomegranate figures in legends and superstitions pretty much around the world. The ancient Hebrews used it in some of their ceremonies, and it supplied a pattern embroidered on the high priest's robe. The curious jagged calix on the fruit was said to have inspired the design of Solomon's crown. It figures frequently in Chinese poetry, and in the Near East its many seeds suggest fertility. Hence, Turkish women are said to practice a form of divination by throwing a Pomegranate upon the ground and deducing the number of children they will have from the number of seeds which will fall out.

The complicated and ramifying legend of Ceres and her daughter Persephone is, of course, the most famous of the legends in which it figures. Carried away to the underworld by Pluto, she might have been redeemed if she had taken no food while in Hades. But because she had eaten one Pomegranate seed she was henceforth compelled to spend half of every year underground. Many interpretations of the story have been given, but some three hundred and fifty years ago, Francis Bacon, who called the Greek myths "elegant and instructive fables", saw in it an allegory of the winter retreat of the vegetable world. Some may think it significant that in our day the only metaphorical use of the fruit is "hand grenade", from the French for Pomegranate.

POMEGRANATE

Punicaceae : Punica

Lychnis

A NUMBER OF WEEDS, *wild flowers, and old-fashioned garden plants are included in the two modern genera of the Pink family called* Lychnis *and* Silene, *by the botanists, Campion and Catchfly in popular speech. The drawings which accompany the two species recorded in the oldest Ms of Dioscorides are so debased by recopying as to be unrecognizable, and Mattioli is justified when he complains that it would be very difficult to distingush between the wild and garden species of which Dioscorides speaks. His own illustration is, on the other hand, obviously from life, and probably represents the Mediterranean species called Rose Campion or* Lychnis coronaria *(L).*

Mattioli comments as follows: "The seed drunk with wine is good against the sting of scorpions. The wild and the garden kinds are very similar. Two drams of the seed taken in wine provoke the evacuation of coleric humours. It is said that scorpions become insensible if this herb is placed near them."

Culpeper introduces his astrological nonsense by assigning Lychnis to Saturn, and adds hopefully that the herb "may be effectual for the plague". On the whole, however, the English Herbalists are more interested in Lychnis as an ornamental than as a medicinal simple and Gerard, after identifying Dioscorides' species as probably Lychnis coronaria, *provides drawings of some dozen different species.*

"The Rose Campion", he writes, "is called Dominararium Rosa . . . Gaza [a fifteenth-century Greek Scholar] translates Lychnis *as Lucernula, because the leaves thereof be soft and fit to make wicks for candles; according to the testimony of Dioscorides it was called* Lychnis, *that is torch . . . according to the signification of the word: clear, bright and light giving flower; and therefore they were called Gardener's Delight or the Gardener's Eye, in Dutch, Christies Eie; in French, Oeillets and Oeillets Dieu; in High Dutch, Marien Roszlin and Himmel Roszlin."*

The Lychnis coronaria *of Dioscorides is common from Maine to New York as an introduced weed. Other wild species are common over the temperate parts of both our East and West as far south as Arizona. As garden plants they are still sometimes grown, but have tended to give way to more sophisticated and spectacular flowers.*

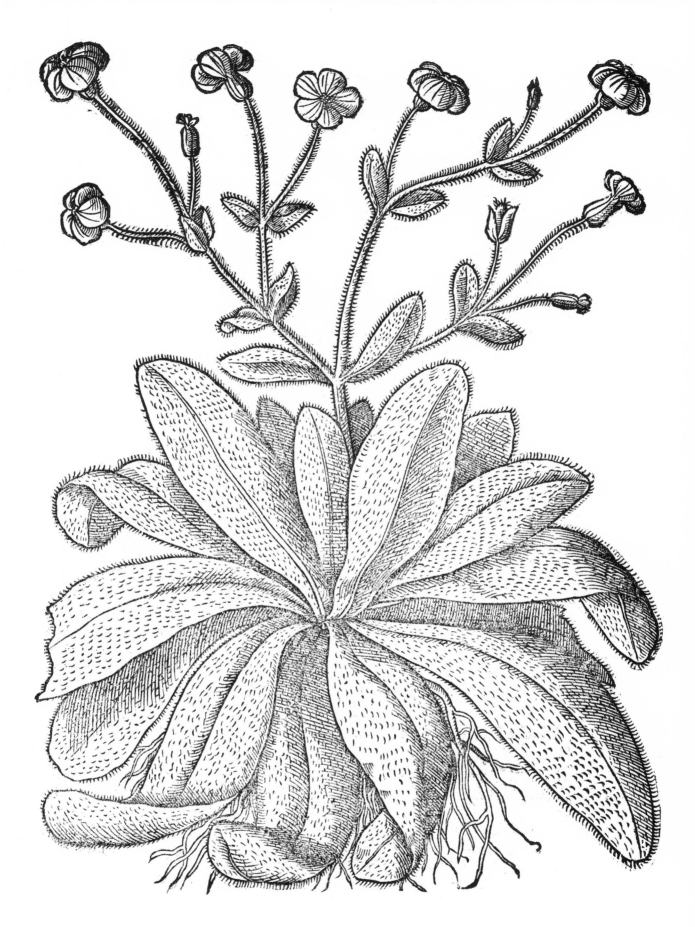

LYCHNIS

Caryophyllaceae: Lychnis

Thorn Apple

"THE ROOT *being drunk with wine in the quantity of a dram has the power to effect not unpleasant fantasies. But two being drunk, make one beside himself for three days, and four being drunk kill him."*

So says Dioscorides, whose "not unpleasant fantasies" must be one of the first recorded references to what we call the hallucinagenic alkaloids. His subject is one of the Daturas, perhaps the Asiatic native known in the Eastern parts of the United States as the Jimson Weed (Datura stramonium). *There are a dozen or more species in all, including the handsome* D. *meteloides of the arid Southwest, and various spectacular tropical species known as Angel Trumpets in Florida and California gardens.*

The Thorn Apple, as the old Herbalists were likely to call it, is a member of the family which includes Tobacco, Belladonna, and the Mandrake, as well as the Tomato and the Red Pepper. Its medicinal, narcotic, hallucinagenic, and poisonous properties are all very real and are still recognized in most pharmacopoeias. It dilates the pupils and, in overdose, produces dizziness and delirium. It was formerly much used, either in the form of powder or in cigarettes, to relieve the spasms of asthma.

Some of the California Indian tribes use it in puberty rites to produce a stupor, and Beverley's History of Virginia *(1705) tells how some soldiers boiled the leaves for a salad, "the effect of which was a very pleasant comedy, for they turned natural fools on it for several days", though in time they recovered without any recollection of what had happened. "Jimson Weed" is a corruption of "Jamestown Weed".*

Gerard speaks of two species, one of which (difficult to identify) "is rare and strange as yet in England", though he raised it from seeds sent him by a learned Herbalist of Paris. He seems to be referring to both sorts when he writes that the Thorn Apple makes a remarkably effective salve to soothe burns "as myself have found by my daily practice, to my great credit and profit".

By 1805, Daturas were well enough established in England for the New Family Herbal *to issue a warning: "A physician has recently seen several children poisoned by the seeds of the Thorn Apple thrown into the street."*

THORN APPLE

Solanaceae : Datura

Almond

THE ALMOND *is a close relative of the Plum and Peach, though we are unlikely to remember the fact because, in this case, we eat the seed and throw the pulp away—unless, like the French and Italians, we have a taste for the whole green fruit.*

It was a native of the Middle East and possibly of the Mediterranean coast, but there is some doubt as to when it was first cultivated widely. Pliny knew it familiarly but doubted that it was known in Italy at the time of Cato, who speaks of "Greek nuts" but may have been referring to something else. At any rate, once it became widely known, it remained a great favorite as a remedy—Pliny lists twenty-nine disorders for which it is recommended—and especially as a luxury food.

Probably typical is an inventory of the household of Jeanne d'Evreux, Queen of France, made in 1372, which lists only twenty pounds of sugar but five hundred pounds of Almonds. Renaissance cookbooks call for it in many recipes and The Modern Herbal *gives one for a seventeenth-century concoction called Almond Milk, which includes Raisins, Sorrel, Violet and Strawberry leaves, Buglose, Endive, Parsnip, Rosemary, and several other herbs, all to be mixed with powdered Almonds.*

Almonds also figure frequently in the legends of various peoples. They are, for instance, mentioned more than once in the Bible, where Aaron's rod was cut from an Almond tree, and in the medieval romance of Tannhauser, whose Almond staff burst into bloom as a sign that his sins had been forgiven. In the story of Attis, we are told that he was conceived when his mother placed an Almond in her bosom.

As for its medical uses, Dioscorides recommends Almonds either taken internally "or laid on as a cataplasm" to "take away spots in the face that were caused by sun burning". This use lingers in cosmetics down to our own time, but most of the Almonds' other supposed virtues have been forgotten, including, I think, the most picturesque of them all as described by Pliny. He reports that five Bitter Almonds (the variety generally preferred in ancient medicine) will prevent intoxication, and cites from Plutarch the story that Drucus, father of the Emperor Tiberius and a notorious drinker, found them a great help.

Incidentally, the Bitter Almond contains a rather large amount of prussic acid and for that reason was early suspected of being dangerous.

ALMOND

Rosaceae : Prunus

Sage

THE REPUTATION *of the common Sage as a sort of wonder drug seems to have arisen in post-classical times and then to have declined, until it now holds a very humble position in the pharmacopoeia. Dioscorides attributes to it a surprisingly short—for him—list of virtues. But during the Middle Ages, and for some authors who came later, it was the indispensable medicine.*

Some thought it owed its extraordinary virtues to the blessing bestowed by the Virgin Mary in gratitude for the fact that, during her flight into Egypt, it gave her shelter from Herod's soldiers. In any case, the Latin name Salvia *is from* salveo, *I save, and a proverb often quoted both in Latin and in the vernacular is the rhetorical question, "How can a man die who has Sage in his garden?"*

After listing the various things Sage is good for, the Herbal of 1525 sums it all up by saying: "Who that useth to eat of this herb or drink it, it is a marvel that any inconvenience should grieve them." Turner also can hardly praise it enough, and Gerard says, "No man needs to doubt of the wholesomeness of Sage ale, being brewed as it should be with Sage, Scabiosa, Betony, Spikenard [no doubt Sweet Cicely], Squinanth [Sweet Rush], and Fennel seeds."

Even today, Sage is probably the most often used seasoning herb. It was so used by the Greeks and the Romans to flavor meat, and during the Middle Ages it turns up very frequently, either alone or with other herbs in recipes for such things as "pig in Sage sauce" and "chickens in hocchee", which latter involves seething the fowl in broth after stuffing it with Sage, Parsley, and Garlic.

Sage was also extremely important as an aid to the freshness and beauty of elegant ladies. Much in medieval life may have been as brutal and untidy as we sometimes assume, but Chaucer's Prioress is often cited as an example of just how delicate and squeamish a fourteenth-century lady could be. And it is interesting to note that about the time when her table manners were being described, the author of The Goodman of Paris *(translated by Eileen Power in 1928) was giving several recipes "for washing the hands at table". One of them, prepared by boiling Sage in water and pouring off the liquid, was to be offered the diners lukewarm.*

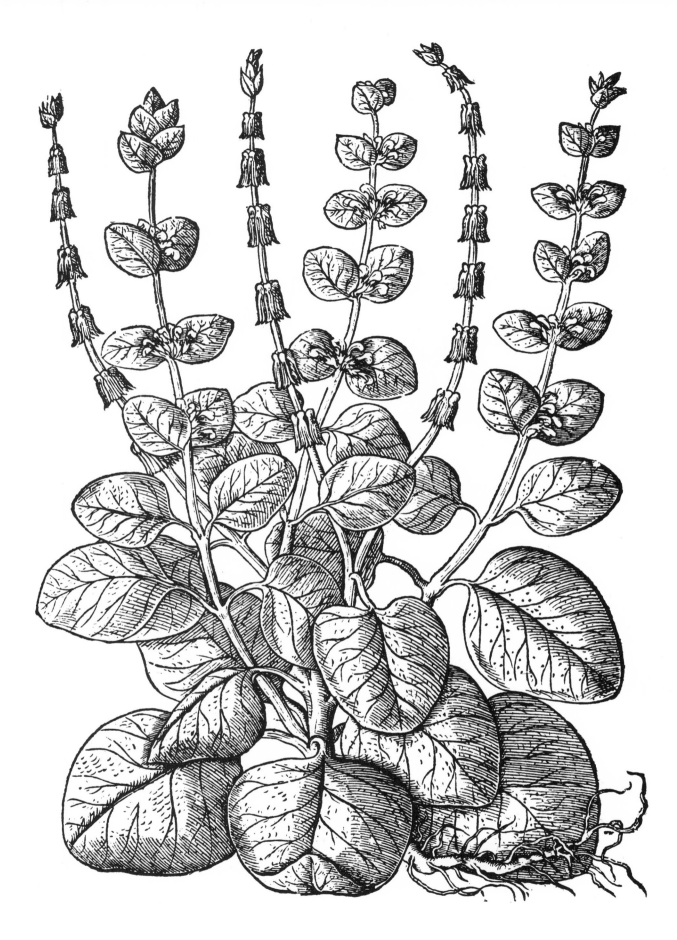

SAGE

Labiatae : Salvia

Broad Bean

THE PEA *or bean family* (Leguminosae) *is one of the largest in the whole plant kingdom, including as it does four or five hundred genera and several thousand species. Some are herbs, some shrubs, some trees, and many, though not all, are climbers. As ornamentals, the family runs a gamut from the Sweet Pea to the great Flame Tree of the tropics.*

It seems clear that what Dioscorides calls Greek Bean is the modern Vicia faba, *which is historically the most important of all, since it is the species which fed whole populations before history began.*

The seventeenth-century gardener Parkinson dismisses it snobbishly as merely "food for the poorer sort", but Henri Fabre (one of the poorer sort himself) pays it a tribute which should be, like Gerard's tribute to the Rose, a classic. Because the idiomatic eloquence of this tribute ought not to be subjected to the indignity of a clumsy translation it is here quoted in the original:

"S'il est un légume du bon Dieu sur la terre, c'est bien le haricot. Il a pour lui toutes les qualités, souplesse de pâte sous la dent, sapidité flatteuse, abondance, bas prix et vertus nutritives. C'est une chair végétale qui, non odieuse, non sanglante, équivaut aux horreurs découpées sur l'étal du boucher. Pour en rappeler énergiquement les services, l'idiome provençal le nomme gounflo-gus.

"Sainte fève, consolation des gueux, à peu de frais, oui, tu le gonfles, le travailleur, l'homme de bien et de talent à qui n'est pas échu le bon numéro dans la loterie insensée de la vie; fève débonnaire, avec trois gouttes d'huile et un filet de vinaigre, tu faisais le régal de mes jeunes années; maintenant encore, sur le tard de mes jours, tu es le bienvenu dans ma pauvre écuelle. Soyons amis jusqu'à la fin."

Dioscorides is less eloquent: "The Greek Bean is windy, flatulent, hard of digestion, causing troublesome dreams; yet good for the cough. . . . It is made less flatulent if the first water in which it was sod [boiled] be cast away; but the green is worse for the stomach and more windy. . . . Being sod in wine it cures inflammations of the stones. And being applied as a cataplasm to the place where the pubes grow in children it keeps them inpuberes a long time. . . . It is applied also to the fluxes of blood occasioned by leeches, being shucked and divided in two parts, according as it grew, and the cut half being closely pressed on."

BROAD BEAN

Leguminosae : Vicia

Hawkweed

THE HAWKWEEDS *compose an enormous genus of something like seven hundred species. Some of them are tall, handsome weeds with orange-red flowers and are therefore occasionally cultivated, though the European species called Orange Hawkweed or Devil's Paintbrush is all too well established as a weed on grasslands in the United States. The popular name is a translation of the first syllable of the technical name, and was given in ancient times because hawks were said to sharpen their eyesight by drinking the sap.*

Mattioli remarks that Hawkweed resembles the wild lettuce—which is right enough since modern botanists put the two in neighboring genera. Dioscorides says it has a cooling and gently binding faculty, hence is good for a burning stomach and, if applied to the skin, for inflammations. Drinking the juice eases gnawing in the stomach and the root helps the bite of the scorpion, if applied to the puncture.

Mattioli adds so many more virtues that he advises keeping the milky juice on hand. Mixed with human milk it cures all maladies of the eye. It serves to counteract all sorts of poison except that which suffocates or affects the bladder. It also induces sleep, facilitates urination, diminishes sexual desire, and increases the supply of blood.

Even this does not complete the list of its virtues. It aids digestion and produces no "crudities" in the stomach. There is nothing which so effectively either increases appetite or diminishes it than this herb, because if one eats very heartily it eases the stomach, and if one eats little it encourages the appetite.

In England, Gerard uses the long-familiar popular name Mouse-ear, presumably a reference to the rough and hairy growth on the leaves, which also "have a small hollowness in them resembling the ear of a mouse, upon which consideration some have called it Myosotis"—which last, by the way, is the botanical name given (for no better reason) to the Forget-me-nots. Gerard then gives us a new kind of virtue for the Mouse-eared Hawkweed: "You steep the herb in water. If steel-edged tools red hot be drenched and cooled therein, oftimes it maketh them so hard that they will cut stone or iron . . . without turning the edge." His method is indeed one in common use for tempering steel, but the herb is usually omitted.

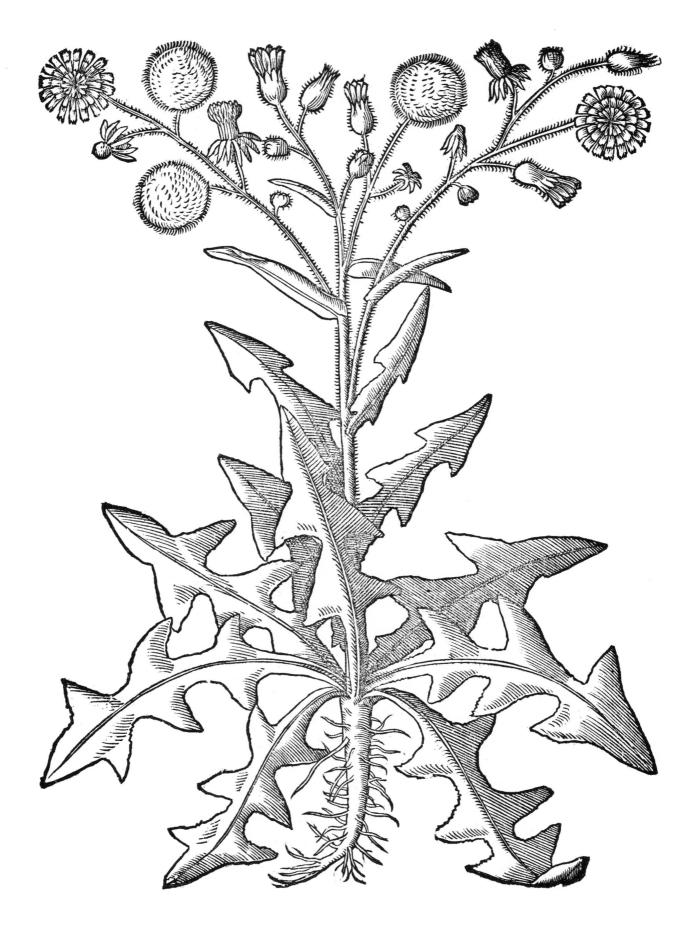

HAWKWEED

Compositae: Hieracium

Medlar

MEDLAR *is the common English name for an edible fruit known to the Greeks and Romans, from whom its modern scientific name* Mespilus *is borrowed. It is a thorny tree, fifteen or twenty feet high, and of Eurasian origin. Though said to be sometimes cultivated in the Northeastern United States and somewhat more commonly in England, it is to most of us completely unfamiliar as a fruit. If known at all, it is known only from garden books or, more likely, as something which turns up frequently in early English literature—largely because of a peculiarity which made it a useful metaphor, especially in moralizing contexts.*

The peculiarity is that the fruit, which is round and said to look somewhat like a brown apple, is very hard and astringent unless kept until decay sets in, at which stage it is pleasantly acid. Hence the metaphor, best illustrated from Shakespeare: "You'll be rotten ere you be half ripe, and that's the right virtue of the Medlar."

Botanically, the Medlar is a member of the huge Rose family and assigned to the subdivision sometimes called the Pyrus *(or Pear) tribe. The flowers are solitary and the top of the fruit is open, so that the stones are easily removed. It was known to Theophrastus, Pliny, and Dioscorides—though Pliny says it is new enough to Southern Italy to have been unknown to Cato (the Elder), who lived during the second and third centuries* B.C. *and wrote on agriculture. Dioscorides, in his few lines devoted to the Medlar, says that it has a round, edible fruit with a broad umbilicus [open end]. Of its medicinal effect, he says only that it is "somewhat binding".*

The English Herbalists and garden writers of the generation following Shakespeare were quite familiar with it. Parkinson describes three varieties which he calls the Greater English, the Lesser English, and the Neopolitan. They are given, he says, "to bind the body . . . yet they are often eaten . . . only for the pleasant sweetness of them when they are made mellow". Culpeper says that they generally flower in May and are ripe in September or October. He assigns them to the influence of Saturn and adds: "A better medicine for strengthening the retentive faculties is hardly to be met with; also it stays the longing of women."

MEDLAR

Rosaceae : Mespilus

Lupine

AMERICANS *know the Lupines as popular garden subjects or (especially in the West) as among the most attractive of wild flowers. In the old world, they were cultivated by the ancient Egyptians as food, and in the Mediterranean region have continued to serve as such to the present day. The beans tend to be bitter but they are very nourishing and extremely rich in protein. Pliny says that no food is more wholesome or easier to digest; also that they produce a cheerful countenance and a fresh complexion.*

A considerable variety of medicinal virtues was attributed to them (Pliny lists thirty-five disorders for which Lupinus *in one form or another is recommended) but their principal real use was, first, as food and, second, as a "green manure". Mattioli says that they were sown "not only for food but also to enrich the soil". He did not, of course, know that, like alfalfa and many other members of the bean family, their roots are capable of fixing atmospheric nitrogen and of supplying it to nitrogen poor soils. He makes the curious statement that Lupines "kill other plants which spring up near them", which may possibly be a misinterpretation of the fact that they flourish in dry, rocky soil where many other wild plants would be unable to survive even if their seeds happened to germinate there.*

The belief that Lupines were good for the skin if taken internally or applied externally lasted well into the eighteenth century and probably much longer. The Toilet of Flora *(1775) gives the following recipe for a foot bath:*

"Take two pounds of Barley, one pound of Rice, three pounds of Lupine, all finely powdered, eight pounds of bran and ten handfuls of Borage and Violet leaves. Boil these ingredients in a sufficient quantity of water. Nothing cleanses . . . the skin as this bath."

Gerard, being as much horticulturist as physician, illustrates four sorts, including the blue and the yellow flowered. He remarks:

"They require (sayeth Theophrastus) a sandy and bad soil; they hardly come up in tilled places, being in their nature wild; they grow in my garden and in other men's gardens about London." Galen, he reminds us, says that "it bringeth down the menses, and expelleth the dead child if it be laid to with myrrhe and honey".

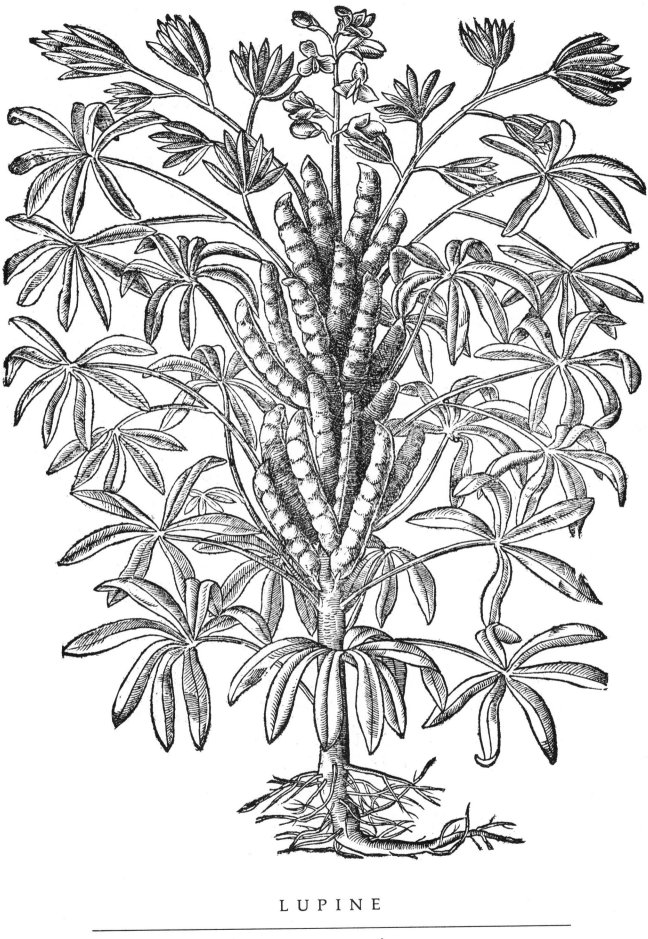

LUPINE

Leguminosae : Lupinus

Tree Ivy

"JUST LIKE THE IVY I'LL CLING TO YOU." *So ran the refrain of at least one popular song. The comparison is a cliché which is one of the oldest and most frequently used of all similes and was already implied when the ancient Greek priest gave a wreath of Ivy to the newly married.*

But Ivy is not only the "clinging vine" par excellence. It was also part of the poet's crown ("Yet once more O ye laurels, and once more/ Yet Myrtles brown and Ivy never seer") as also of the crown of Bacchus and his troupe ("The Ivy falls from the Bacchanale's hair/ Over her eyebrows hiding her eyes"). And it was probably the association with Bacchus that is responsible for the ancient belief that a crown of Ivy tended to protect against intoxication.

Pliny mentions twenty-three kinds of Ivy and there are innumerable recognized by gardeners today, though most of them are probably only horticultural varieties of Hedera helix, *which is commonly called English Ivy despite the fact that it is no commoner in England than in Europe. Even the Tree Ivy illustrated here is probably not a distinct species, though it was already noted by Pliny who writes: "There is an Ivy also which grows upright and stands without support, being the only one that does so . . ." (An anticipatory symbol of the feminist, perhaps.)*

Mattioli describes in detail the aerial rootlets by which Ivy attaches itself, but seems to suppose that it is a parasite. From walls as well as from trees, so he believed, it draws into itself all the moisture and for this reason will continue to grow if cut off at the ground. All of this is, of course, mistaken. Ivy may sometimes smother a tree but it draws nothing from it.

As for its medicinal virtues, Mattioli writes: "All the Ivys are bitter and astringent and weaken the nerves. The flowers taken with wine three times a day are a singularly effective remedy against dysentery . . . The juice of Ivy or its berries enfeebles the body and troubles the spirit if one drinks too much . . . Five grains of Ivy roasted with the rind of the Pomegranate . . . eases the pain of toothache if poured into the ear opposite the painful tooth. The berries will dye the hair black."

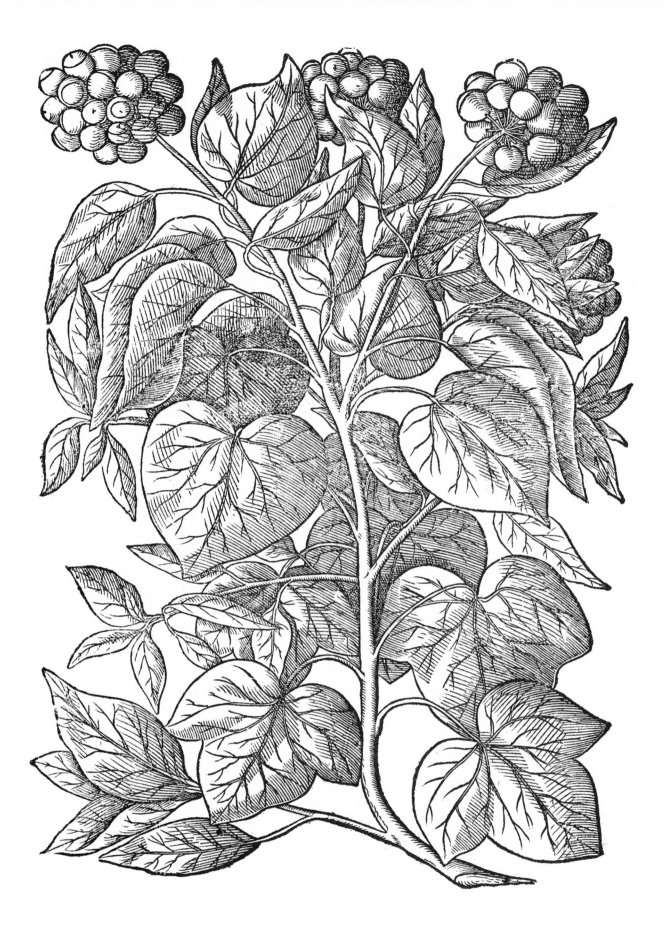

TREE IVY

Araliaceae : Hedera

Plantain

HOMELY PLANTAIN *shares with handsome Dandelion the bitterest fury of the suburbanite proud of his lawn. Mattioli pictures three species, of which the one he calls The Great Plantain apparently represents* P. major, *the very unwanted immigrant from Europe which will grow luxuriantly while grass turns brown and dies.*

Most of the perhaps two hundred species in the family are weedy herbs, some occasionally used as pot herbs, but otherwise of minimal ornamental or utilitarian value. Despite the fact that they are insipidly innocent and probably without any physiological effect they were (possibly because harmless placebos) favorites with Herbalists. They appear not only in Dioscorides but in the very earliest records of Anglo-Saxon medicine, as well as in the rather skimpy Herbal of 1525. They also figure in the folklore of various peoples and are said to be known to the aborigines of Australia, New Zealand, and the United States by names translatable as "white man's foot", in reference to introduction by Europeans.

Gerard writes: "I find in ancient writers many goodmorrows, which I think not meet to bring into memory again: as that three roots [of the Plantain] will cure one grief, four another disease, six hanged about the neck are good for another malady, etc., all of which are but ridiculous toys."

More than half a century later Culpeper was, nevertheless, calling on his freewheeling astrology to support extravagant claims.

Characteristically, he arbitrarily assigns plants to one or another of the planets, assigns "influences" to these planets, and then explains the alleged actions of his "simples" as either by "sympathy" or "antipathy", thus giving himself leave to say pretty much anything he likes about the "virtues" of any herb. Of Plantain: "It is under the command of Venus and cures the head by antipathy to Mars and the privities by sympathy to Venus; neither is there hardly a martial disease but it cures . . . . The plantains are singularly good wound herbs, to heal fresh or old wounds or sores either inward or outward." (No doubt in antipathy to Mars.)

Plantain is also good against consumption, dropsy, falling sickness, jaundice, deafness, cancers or sores of the mouth or privy parts, piles, etc., etc.

PLANTAIN

Plantaginaceae: Plantago

Mallow

THE MALLOWS *compose an enormous cosmopolitan family of more than forty genera and some nine hundred species. Among them are the Hollyhock and the Marshmallow, a member of the same genus (Althaea) as the garden Hollyhock. The roots of the Marshmallow furnished the mucilaginous juice used in making what is the Girl Scouts' favorite confection until Gum Arabic became a cheaper substitute, and gelatin, in turn, a cheaper substitute for Gum Arabic.*

Dioscorides mentions only two species of Mallow, the wild and the cultivated. Mattioli illustrates what are probably the same two—presumably Malva sylvestra *and the Hollyhock which we now put in the genus* Althea. *He recognizes, however, that there are many different sorts. He also cites a remark of Theophrastus to the effect that many plants grow much larger when moved from the fields to the garden, and points to certain Mallows grown around the baths at Lixus (a town in North Africa), which are so magnificent that the garden where they grow is believed to have been the original garden of the Hesperides. Describing what he calls the Great Mallow (probably our Hollyhock), he says: "Its flower is large, resembles a rose, is leafy and of various colors; some being a flamboyant purplish red, others white, still others flesh colored; and in form as well as color so like a Rose that one would call it such except that it has no odor."*

The Mallows have long been eaten by many peoples as a pot herb, and modern research has revealed that at least some species are very rich in vitamins. Medical uses were mostly connected with the emollient juice in the roots of many species and these uses were widely varied as well as numerous. Several American Indian tribes employed Mallow as do the Mexicans, from whom we translate the popular name of a common Southwestern species "Sore-eye Poppy".

Mattioli, closely following Dioscorides, writes:

"The raw leaves mashed with a little salt and honey cure the fistulas in the eyes which come close to the nose . . . Applied to the stings of the wasp or honey-flies [bees], they are very good; and whoever will wash them with oil and anoint himself with this composition will be protected against both wasps and honey-flies . . . Cooked and mixed with oil and applied to Saint Anthony's Fire [erysipelas] as burns, it cures them."

MALLOW

Malvaceae : Malva

Licorice

MOST OF US *probably first met Licorice as the flavoring in rubbery "penny candies" moulded into various fanciful shapes. Unless we had also met it in the form of the straight, pencil-sized segments of root which old-fashioned drugstores stocked and unsophisticated children chewed, we probably took Licorice as a fact of life without inquiring where it came from. Actually, the plant is a member of the bean family; its English name is a corruption of the Greek Glycyrrhiza (sweet root); and it has been known at least since classical times.*

The Romans are said to have got it from the Scythians, but in Dioscorides' day it was commonly grown in Italy for its medicinal uses and also as an ornamental semi-shrub with pea-like blossoms.

Licorice still figures in modern pharmacopoeia, where it is recommended for the same purposes as suggested by Theophrastus, Hippocrates, Pliny, Dioscorides, and most other Herbalists: that is, to soothe an irritated throat—a use which made the bearded Smith Brothers better known in the United States than many more illustrious citizens of their time.

As usual, the ancients attributed to Licorice other virtues no longer recognized. Pliny says that "so long as a person keeps it in his mouth he will never experience hunger or thirst", and Theophrastus declares that the Scythians were able to live eleven or twelve days on a decoction of Licorice and a cheese made of mare's milk.

Though Licorice can be grown in the United States, we ordinarily import it from Europe or Asia. Since it is mentioned by Turner and, later, by Gerard and Culpeper, it must have been cultivated in England at least as far back as the sixteenth century. Gerard says: "These plants [there are several species, but only G. glabra is of commercial importance] grow wild in several places in Germany, France, and Spain, but they are planted in gardens in England, whereof my garden hath plenty; the poor people of the north parts of England do manure it with great diligence whereby they obtain great plenty thereof, replanting the same only in three or four years."

Today, Licorice is added to the malt beverage called Porter and is, of course, a flavoring in both chewing and some smoking tobaccos.

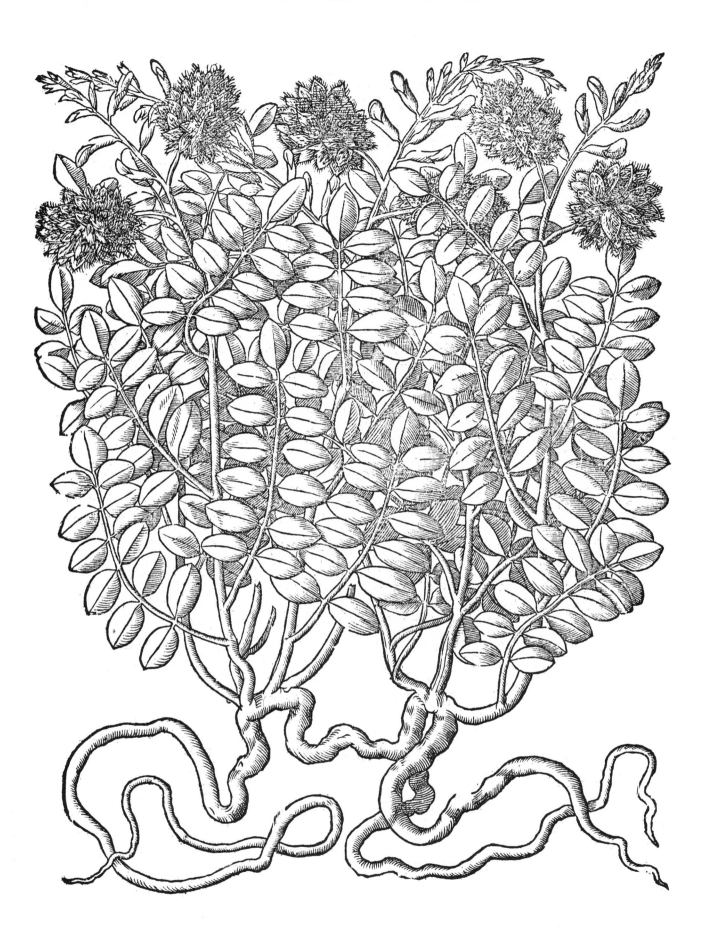

LICORICE

Glycyrrhiza

Wormwood

TO MOST AMERICANS, *"Vermouth" will suggest "Martini" not "Vermifuge", but the latter would be more reasonable since the word refers to worms and to the use of several species of the herb to expel them from the human body. Dioscorides was well aware of their effectiveness for this purpose; the common English name Wormwood also refers to it; and one species is still an official remedy in the U.S. Dispensary. The popular culinary herb Tarragon (also called Estragon) belongs to the same genus and so does the Sagebrush of the Western plains. The species illustrated here is the modern* Artemesia cina.

The modern Artmesia absinthium *is the potent ingredient in the alcoholic liquor called Absinthe, and something of the sort was obviously known to the ancients, since Pliny writes: "There is made of it also a wine which is called Absinthe which they use in the absence of a fever . . . and otherwise also they drink to each other of it in the summer, thinking it to be a causer of health."*

As a medicine, Dioscorides recommends it for a long list of disorders including dullness of sight, pains in the ears, delayed menstruation, and poisonous bites of "the shrew mouse and the dragon of the sea". You may also use it to hang in clothes chests to preserve them from insect pests and you may make of it an ink which will prevent mice from destroying the manuscripts written with it. He adds the warning that drunk as a potion the juice is bad for the stomach and will cause headache. Modern medicine tells us that the drink of evil reputation can, because of the Wormwood flavoring, cause serious nervous disorders.

An English herbal of about the year 1000 (the so-called Apuleius Platonicus) informs us that Wormwood was discovered by Diana, who gave it to the Centaur Chiron, founder of medicine. It also recommends the traveler to carry a bit of the herb with him if he wishes to avoid feeling the fatigues of a journey. And since superstitions are long-enduring, it has been reported that as late as 1925 a driver along the dangerous road leading to Malaga had a sprig of Wormwood hanging from his windshield—in lieu, perhaps, of a St. Christopher medal.

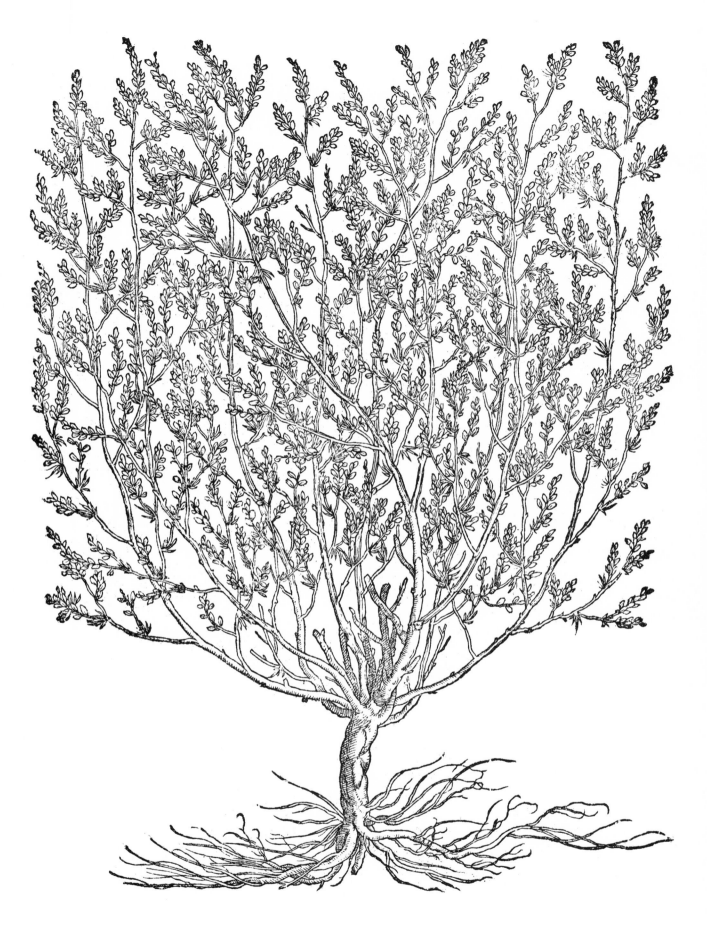

WORMWOOD

Compositae : Artemisia

Woad

THOSE OLD ENOUGH *to remember the days when Caesar's* Gallic Wars *was obligatory reading in every high school may recall that the Britons of Caesar's day were accustomed—men and women alike—to paint themselves all over with a blue dye called Glastum or Woad. The custom was curious enough to be referred to by Pliny also, though no one seemed to know whether it had something to do with religion or was intended merely to make the Britons look more terrifying in battle.*

It was only the use, not the plant itself, that was unfamiliar to the Romans. This member of the Mustard family had been known for centuries as the source of the purple dye most commonly used. The other purple dyes were made from the galls on the Kermes Oak (see page 208) and the marine gastropod Murex, from which came the famous Royal or Tyrian Purple. But the former, as Pliny tells us, was used only for the uniforms of certain high military officers and the Murex was so much a luxury item that it inspired him with one of his characteristic outbursts of rhetorical moralizing. The collectors of the dye plant are fortunate, he says, because "they do not have to seek the Murex at the bottom of the sea, or to expose themselves to the prey of the monsters of the deep while tearing it from their jaws . . . and all this for the purpose of finding the means whereby some mother of a family may appear more charming in the eyes of her paramour, or the seducer may make himself more captivating to the wife of another man".

The use of Woad in medicine appears to have been minor, and both Parkinson and Culpeper refer skeptically to the belief that the plant is fatal to bees. This plant continued to be the principal source of blue dye until the opening of a sea route to India made Indigo, a member of the Pea family, readily accessible. For a time, attempts were made to protect the home grown product by laws forbidding the importation of Indigo, but the attempt was abandoned during the eighteenth century. Then the invention of the anilines put Indigo into second rank. Here we have another typical case of a process whereby a native plant or other natural product is replaced, first by an exotic, and then by an artificial product.

WOAD

Cruciferae : Isatis

Teasel

IN 1530, *the Worshipful Clothworker's Company of London was granted arms described by the Herald as "sable, a chevron ermine, between two habbicks [a clothworker's tool] in chief, and a Teasel in base, proper". Nothing could be more appropriate than the last item which is, of course, the European Teasel whose prickly seed heads were long used (and still are used) in "fulling", that is, in raising the nap on woolen cloths.*

The Herbalists put the Teasel with the Thistles because it is prickly, but it is now assigned to a different family, of which the only other members of either commercial or ornamental importance are the Scabiosas. The Fuller's Teasel (D. fullonum) is native to Southern Europe but was long ago introduced into England, where it is said to be found as an escape, especially near woolen mills. It was brought to the United States in 1840 and is said to be a rather rare escape here—as are also two other European species.

Turner, conspicuous among the Herbalists for adding pleasant little touches, remarks that, "In the beginning of winter the goldfinches use much to haunt this herb for the sake of the seeds whereof they are very desirous".

Dioscorides passes on the legend that "the worms of the heads being bound up in a purse and hanged about the neck or the arm are said to cure such as have quartanes [fevers]". Pliny is responsible for passing on the further information that these same worms should be rubbed on the teeth or imbedded in wax and then inserted in a hollow tooth—presumably to cure its aching. These superstitions went down the ages along with the use of the Teasel by fullers, and Gerard works himself into high indignation to find such old wives' tales still flourishing.

It is needless, he says, to repeat the beliefs which Pliny reports concerning the worms or maggots commonly found in Teasel heads. That these beliefs are nothing else but vain and trifling toys he himself has demonstrated by experiment. When he had a long continued fever he was persuaded by fantastic acquaintances to try all sorts of charms, including Teasel worms hung about his neck, spiders in a Walnut shell etc., etc. "Notwithstanding, I say, my help came from God himself, for these medicines and all other such things did me no good at all."

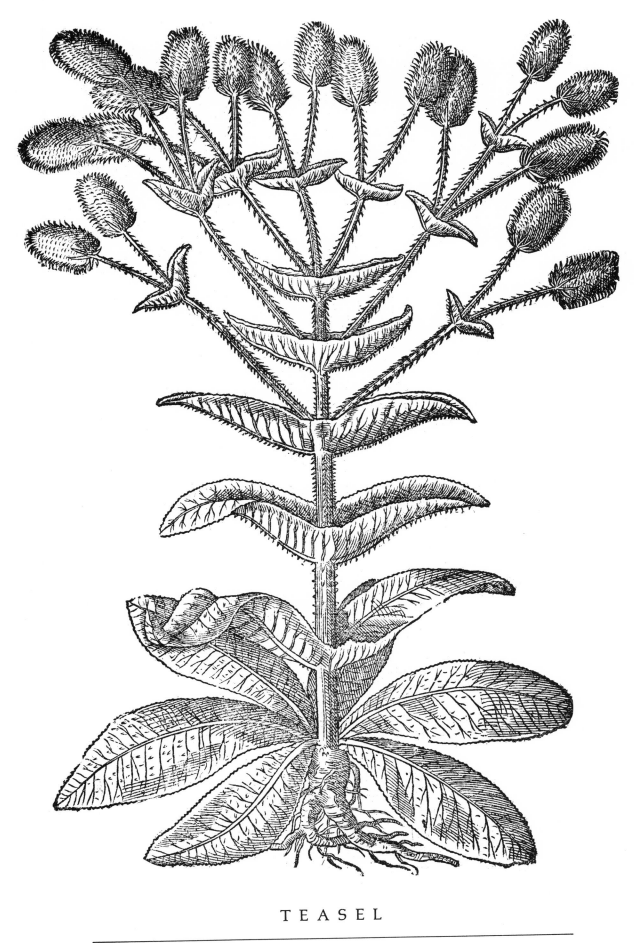

TEASEL

Dipsacaceae : Dipsacus

Capsicum

THIS IS *one of the pseudo-Peppers and was contributed by the New World. Mattioli sounds a bit apologetic for his classification, for he begins with: "We put also among the Peppers this kind which we call Indian Pepper because its taste is very biting and sharp. We also still call the Capsicums 'Pepper'."*

This misnaming is another illustration of the way in which the Herbalists fumbled because they could not fix upon any one characteristic or group of characteristics as significant for classification. Thus, they put the Acanthus with the Thistles just because both were spiny, and Oxalis with the Clovers just because both have three leaflets to a leaf-stem— and all despite the fact that in a dozen other respects Acanthus and Thistle or Oxalis and Clover have as little in common as the true Peppers and the Capsicums.

Mattioli remarks in passing that there are various species of Peppers differing in their fruits. There are, of course, many more kinds than he was familiar with, since the same genus includes all the hot and all the sweet Green or Red Peppers, of which all but one are of the Western hemisphere. The genus belongs to the versatile Tomato-Potato family and includes also the poisonous Belladona, Henbane, Tobacco, and even the Mandrake. The first recorded mention of a Capsicum dates from 1494, when a physician accompanying Columbus refers to it as a condiment.

Mattioli hardly distinguishes the "virtues" of the Red Peppers from those of the true ones, but, speaking only of the Red, he says: "They are hot to the fourth degree; as the result of which fact they burn and ulcerate.

Modern medicine continues to recognize the Red Peppers as having certain limited uses as a carminative, stimulant, and rubefacient—which last means, as the learned will recognize, "a maker red"—and it has much the same effect and use as mustard. Capsicum is also sometimes given to arrest diarrhea. In the folk medicine of the American Southwest and Mexico its uses are more varied. There it is good against the ague, and if small Peppers are swallowed whole they will cure a cold. They are also said to be a very strong aphrodisiac, though the number of things credited with this characteristic suggests that a ready spontaneity is often attributed to some artificial stimulant.

CAPSICUM

Solanaceae : Capsicum

Bibliography

The following books and authors are frequently quoted or cited in the text:

Banckes' Herbal. (1525). The first printed Herbal in English. So-called from the name of its printer. Author or compiler unknown.

COLES, WILLIAM. A fellow of New College, Oxford, who was himself an ardent collector of herbs but whose *Adam in Eden* (1657) was old-fashioned in its reliance upon the Doctrine of Signatures.

CULPEPER, NICHOLAS. Astrologer and unorthodox physician who began his practice in London about 1640 and carried on a continuous feud with the College of Physicians, whom he denounced as proud, insulting, and domineering dunces. Despite the absurd pseudo-logic of his astrological method which permitted him to "prove" almost anything he wished, he nevertheless claimed to be superior to all his predecessors and all the orthodox physicians because he alone is always guided by "reason". His book, published under various titles, was repeatedly reprinted (probably chiefly for the benefit of those who undertook to treat their own illnesses) and has survived in condensed form down to our own day.

DIOSCORIDES, PEDANIUS. Greek physician who was born in Asia Minor and flourished about 40-70 A.D. Little is known of him except through his work which is sometimes called "De Materia Medica" and which continued, at least down into the seventeenth century, to be regarded as the fountainhead of botanical knowledge. The oldest surviving Ms is Byzantine of the sixth century A.D. and is illustrated by what appear to be very much debased copies of earlier pictures. Dioscorides was translated into English in 1655 by one John Goodyear and it is this translation (spelling somewhat modernized) which is quoted in the preceding pages.

GERARD, JOHN. *The Herbal; or General History of Plants.* (1597). A barber-surgeon passionately interested in horticulture who had his own garden in London and also supervised that of Lord Burghley. His book is perhaps the most famous of the English Herbals and the handsomest—a folio, some copies of which have hand-colored illustrations. It is actually but unadmittedly based very largely on the work of the Belgian botanist Rembert Dodoens.

Herbarius zu Teutsch. (1485). Perhaps the most important of the early German Herbals. Author unknown.

Hortus Sanitatis. (1491). Based on the preceding item but well-known in a French translation from the original Latin.

MATTIOLI, PIERANDREA. *Commentaries on the Six Books of Dioscorides.* First published in Latin in 1544. Later translated into several languages and appearing in some fifty different editions. The author was a distinguished medical practitioner who became physician to the Emperor Maxmilian II. He died of the plague while functioning as one of the official physicians during an outbreak in Lyons. His great work with (in some editions) superb illustrations is much more ambitious than the title would suggest. New plants and many new species of the genera mentioned by Dioscorides are included and much attention is given to identification. Perhaps the most imposing of all the Herbals.

PLINY, GAIUS SECUNDUS. *Natural History.* Pliny the Elder was a garrulous, enthusiastic, and completely uncritical Roman gentleman who, with the aid of a secretary, summarized and digested into an enormous compendium all that he could find in previous authors about plants, animals, minerals, geography, etc. He claims to have stated twenty thousand facts drawn from two thousand books by one hundred authors. Since most of his authorities have perished, his collection is our richest source of information concerning the knowledge and beliefs of the western world during the classic period. Pliny himself was killed during the destruction of Pompeii by an eruption of Vesuvius in 79 A.D. Despite (and partly because of) its admixture of tall tales and superstitious nonsense, the *Natural History* makes delightful reading.

PARKINSON, JOHN. *Paradisi in Sole Paradisus Terrestris.* (1629). The title of this work is a farfetched bi-lingual pun on the author's name. His own London garden was famous and he held the title of Herbalist to Charles I. His book is concerned largely with gardening for pleasure rather than merely for utility.

Pseudo-Apuleius. Name commonly given to a primitive Herbal by an unidentified compiler. It is based largely on Dioscorides and Pliny and may have existed in manuscript since late classical times.

THEOPHRASTUS. Treatise on plants. Aristotle's writings on plants have been lost. Those of Theophrastus are, therefore, the earliest to survive from the great age of Greece. For thirty-five years he conducted the school of philosophy which his mentor had founded with great success. How much of his Treatise derives from Aristotle can only be guessed, but its method is Aristotelian. It is sometimes called "philosophical botany" because its primary concern is with generalizations concerning the nature of plant life rather than with either medicine or systematics.

TURNER, WILLIAM. *New Herbal.* (1551-1568). A somewhat eccentric clergyman whose strong dissenting opinions brought him into conflict with the Church of England authorities and made him a fugitive during the reign of Mary. He had taken a medical degree in Italy and was at one time physician to the Duke of Somerset. He traveled widely in England to observe plants in the field and his originality has earned him the title of Father of English Botany.

From the standpoint of the science of botany as opposed to gardening, the most important early English works are that by JOHN RAY (which has been mentioned in the Introduction) and (nearly half a century earlier) SIR THOMAS BROWNE's *Pseudodoxia Epidemica; or Vulgar Errors* (1646), which devotes considerable attention to common errors concerning plants, although it sometimes accepts one erroneous opinion while rejecting another.

Among books of the eighteenth, nineteenth, and twentieth centuries which illustrate a continuing interest in what might be called the Herbalist's approach may be mentioned: *Botanicum Officinale; or A Compengous Herbal Giving an Account of All Such Plants As Are Now Used in the Practice of Physic* by JOSEPH MILLER (1722); *A New Family Herbal or Popular Account of the Nature and Properties of the Various Plants Used in Medicine, Diet and the Arts* by ROBERT JOHN THORNTON, M.D. (1810); *A Modern Herbal* by M. GRIEVE, with an introduction by the editor, Mrs. C. F. Leyel, (1931).

Of the many recent books dealing with herbs and related subjects, the following are among those most useful and interesting:

ARBER, AGNES. *Herbals; Their Origin and Evolution.* (1938).

DAY, AVANELLE and STUCKEY, LILLIE. *The Spice Cookbook.* (1964).

FOX, HELEN. *Gardening with Herbs.* (1936).

FREEMAN, MARGARET. *Herbs for the Medieval Household.* (1943).

JAGENDORF, M. A. *Folk Wines, Cordials, and Brandies.* (1963).

KREIG, MARGARET B. *Green Medicine.* (1964).

ROHDE, ELEANOR. *The Old English Herbals.* (1922).

Index

*Plants that are illustrated have a bold number for the page
on which the commentary facing the Plate appears.*

254